Outlook 2010: Advanced

Instructor's Edition

Outlook 2010: Advanced

President, Axzo Press:	Jon Winder
Vice President, Product Development:	Charles G. Blum
Vice President, Operations:	Josh Pincus
Director of Publishing Systems Development:	Dan Quackenbush
Developmental Editor:	Tim Poulsen
Copyeditor:	Catherine Oliver
Keytester:	Cliff Coryea

Trademarks

ILT Series is a trademark of Axzo Press.

Some of the product names and company names used in this book have been used for identification purposes only and may be trademarks or registered trademarks of their respective manufacturers and sellers.

Disclaimer

We reserve the right to revise this publication and make changes from time to time in its content without notice.

ISBN 10: 1-4260-2121-6
ISBN 13: 978-1-4260-2121-3

Printed in the United States of America

1 2 3 4 5 6 7 8 9 10 GL 13 12 11

What is the Microsoft ® Office Specialist Program?

The Microsoft Office Specialist Program enables candidates to show that they have something exceptional to offer – proven expertise in certain Microsoft programs. Recognized by businesses and schools around the world, over 4 million certifications have been obtained in over 100 different countries. The Microsoft Office Specialist Program is the only Microsoft-approved certification program of its kind.

What is the Microsoft Office Specialist Certification?

The Microsoft Office Specialist certification validates through the use of exams that you have obtained specific skill sets within the applicable Microsoft Office programs and other Microsoft programs included in the Microsoft Office Specialist Program. The candidate can choose which exam(s) they want to take according to which skills they want to validate.

The available Microsoft Office Specialist Program exams include*:
- Using Windows Vista®
- Using Microsoft® Office Word 2007
- Using Microsoft® Office Word 2007 - Expert
- Using Microsoft® Office Excel® 2007
- Using Microsoft® Office Excel® 2007 - Expert
- Using Microsoft® Office PowerPoint® 2007
- Using Microsoft® Office Access® 2007
- Using Microsoft® Office Outlook® 2007
- Using Microsoft SharePoint® 2007

The Microsoft Office Specialist Program 2010 exams will include*:
- Microsoft Word 2010
- Microsoft Word 2010 Expert
- Microsoft Excel® 2010
- Microsoft Excel® 2010 Expert
- Microsoft PowerPoint® 2010
- Microsoft Access® 2010
- Microsoft Outlook® 2010
- Microsoft SharePoint® 2010

What does the Microsoft Office Specialist Approved Courseware logo represent?

The logo indicates that this courseware has been approved by Microsoft to cover the course objectives that will be included in the relevant exam. It also means that after utilizing this courseware, you may be better prepared to pass the exams required to become a certified Microsoft Office Specialist.

For more information:

To learn more about Microsoft Office Specialist exams, visit www.microsoft.com/learning/msbc

To learn about other Microsoft approved courseware from Axzo Press, visit http://www.axzopress.com.

Contents

Introduction

After reading this introduction, you'll know how to:

A Use ILT Series manuals in general.

B Use prerequisites, a target student description, course objectives, and a skills inventory to properly set students' expectations for the course.

C Set up a classroom to teach this course.

D Get support for setting up and teaching this course.

Topic A: About the manual

ILT Series philosophy

Our goal is to make you, the instructor, as successful as possible. To that end, our manuals facilitate students' learning by providing structured interaction with the software itself. While we provide text to help you explain difficult concepts, the hands-on activities are the focus of our courses. Leading the students through these activities will teach the skills and concepts effectively.

We believe strongly in the instructor-led class. For many students, having a thinking, feeling instructor in front of them will always be the most comfortable way to learn. Because the students' focus should be on you, our manuals are designed and written to facilitate your interaction with the students, and not to call attention to manuals themselves.

We believe in the basic approach of setting expectations, then teaching, and providing summary and review afterwards. For this reason, lessons begin with objectives and end with summaries. We also provide overall course objectives and a course summary to provide both an introduction to and closure on the entire course.

Our goal is your success. We encourage your feedback in helping us to continually improve our manuals to meet your needs.

Manual components

The manuals contain these major components:

- Table of contents
- Introduction
- Units
- Course summary
- Glossary
- Index

Each element is described below.

Table of contents

The table of contents acts as a learning roadmap for you and the students.

Introduction

The introduction contains information about our training philosophy and our manual components, features, and conventions. It contains target student, prerequisite, objective, and setup information for the specific course. Finally, the introduction contains support information.

Units

Units are the largest structural component of the actual course content. A unit begins with a title page that lists objectives for each major subdivision, or topic, within the unit. Within each topic, conceptual and explanatory information alternates with hands-on activities. Units conclude with a summary, comprising one paragraph for each topic, and an independent practice activity that gives students an opportunity to practice the skills they've learned.

The conceptual information takes the form of text paragraphs, exhibits, lists, and tables. The activities are structured in two columns, one telling students what to do, the other providing explanations, descriptions, and graphics. Throughout a unit, instructor notes are found in the left margin.

Course summary

This section provides a text summary of the entire course. It's useful for providing closure at the end of the course. The course summary also indicates the next course in this series, if there is one, and lists additional resources students might find useful as they continue to learn about the software.

Glossary

The glossary provides definitions for all of the key terms used in this course.

Index

The index at the end of this manual makes it easy for you and your students to find information about a particular software component, feature, or concept.

Manual conventions

We've tried to keep the number of elements and the types of formatting to a minimum in the manuals. We think this approach aids in clarity and makes the manuals more classically elegant. But there are some conventions and icons you should know about.

Convention	Description
Italic text	In conceptual text, indicates a new term or feature.
Bold text	In unit summaries, indicates a key term or concept. In an independent practice activity, indicates an explicit item that you select, choose, or type.
`Code font`	Indicates code or syntax.

`Longer strings of ▶`
`code will look ▶`
`like this.`
	In the hands-on activities, any code that's too long to fit on a single line is divided into segments by one or more continuation characters (▶). This code should be entered as a continuous string of text.

	In the left margin, provide tips, hints, and warnings for the instructor.
Select **bold item**	In the left column of hands-on activities, bold sans-serif text indicates an explicit item that you select, choose, or type.
Keycaps like (↵ ENTER)	Indicate a key on the keyboard you must press.
	Warnings prepare instructors for potential classroom management problems.
	Tips give extra information the instructor can share with students.
	Setup notes provide a realistic business context for instructors to share with students or indicate additional setup steps required for the current activity.
	Projector notes indicate that there's a PowerPoint slide for the adjacent content.

Instructor note/icon (column header at left)

Instructor notes.

⚠ _Warning icon._

TIPS✓ _Tip icon._

⬡ _Setup icon._

◰ _Projector icon._

Hands-on activities

The hands-on activities are the most important parts of our manuals. They're divided into two primary columns. The "Here's how" column gives short directions to the students. The "Here's why" column provides explanations, graphics, and clarifications. To the left, instructor notes provide tips, warnings, setups, and other information for the instructor only. Here's a sample:

Do it!

A-1: Creating a commission formula

Here's how	Here's why
1 Open Sales	This is an oversimplified sales compensation worksheet. It shows sales totals, commissions, and incentives for five sales reps.
2 Observe the contents of cell F4	[F4 ▼] [= =E4*C_Rate] The commission rate formulas use the name "C_Rate" instead of a value for the commission rate.

Take the time to make sure your students understand this worksheet. We'll be here a while.

For these activities, we've provided a collection of data files designed to help students learn each skill in a real-world business context. As students work through the activities, they'll modify and update these files. Of course, students might make a mistake and therefore want to re-key the activity starting from scratch. To make it easy to start over, students rename each data file at the end of the first activity in which the file is modified. Our convention for renaming files is to add the word "My" to the beginning of the file name. In the above activity, for example, students are using a file called "Sales" for the first time. At the end of this activity, they save the file as "My sales," thus leaving the "Sales" file unchanged. If students make mistakes, they can start over using the original "Sales" file.

In some activities, however, it may not be practical to rename the data file. Such exceptions are indicated with an instructor note. If students want to retry one of these activities, you need to provide a fresh copy of the original data file.

PowerPoint presentations

Each unit in this course has an accompanying PowerPoint presentation. These slide shows are designed to support your classroom instruction while providing students with a visual focus. Each presentation begins with a list of unit objectives and ends with a unit summary slide. We strongly recommend that you run these presentations from the instructor's station as you teach this course. A copy of PowerPoint Viewer is included, so it is not necessary to have PowerPoint installed on your computer.

The ILT Series PowerPoint add-in

The CD also contains a PowerPoint add-in that enables you to do two things:

- Create slide notes for the class
- Display a control panel for the Flash movies embedded in the presentations

To load the PowerPoint add-in:

1 Copy the Course_ILT.ppa file to a convenient location on your hard drive.
2 Start PowerPoint.
3 Choose Tools, Macro, Security to open the Security dialog box. On the Security Level tab, select Medium (if necessary), and then click OK.
4 Choose Tools, Add-Ins to open the Add-Ins dialog box. Then, click Add New.
5 Browse to and double-click the Course_ILT.ppa file, and then click OK. A message box will appear, warning you that macros can contain viruses.
6 Click Enable Macros. The Course_ILT add-in should now appear in the Available Add-Ins list (in the Add-Ins dialog box). The "x" in front of Course_ILT indicates that the add-in is loaded.
7 Click Close to close the Add-Ins dialog box.

After you complete this procedure, a new toolbar will be available at the top of the PowerPoint window. This toolbar contains a single button labeled "Create SlideNotes." Click this button to generate slide-notes files in both text (.txt) and Excel (.xls) format. By default, these files will be saved to the folder that contains the presentation. If the PowerPoint file is on a CD-ROM or in some other location to which the slide-notes files cannot be saved, you will be prompted to save the presentation to your hard drive and try again.

When you run a presentation and come to a slide that contains a Flash movie, you will see a small control panel in the lower-left corner of the screen. You can use this panel to start, stop, and rewind the movie, or to play it again.

Topic B: Setting student expectations

Properly setting students' expectations is essential to your success. This topic will help you do that by providing:

- Prerequisites for this course
- A description of the target student
- A list of the objectives for the course
- A skills assessment for the course

Course prerequisites

Students taking this course should be familiar with personal computers and the use of a keyboard and a mouse. Furthermore, this course assumes that students have completed the following courses or have equivalent experience:

- *Windows 7: Basic*, *Windows Vista: Basic*, or *Windows XP: Basic*
- *Outlook 2010: Basic*
- *Outlook 2010: Intermediate*

Target student

The target student for this course should know the basics of using Microsoft Outlook 2010. Students will get the most out of this course if their goal is to learn advanced techniques for managing the mailbox, create notes and Journal entries, share Outlook content, and customize mail templates. Candidates for the Microsoft Office Specialist Outlook 2010 certification are the primary target students for this course.

Course objectives

You should share these overall course objectives with your students at the beginning of the day. This gives the students an idea about what to expect, and it helps you identify students who might be misplaced. Students are considered misplaced when they lack the prerequisite knowledge or when they already know most of the subject matter to be covered.

Note: In addition to the general objectives listed below, specific Microsoft Office Specialist exam objectives are listed at the beginning of each topic (where applicable) and are highlighted by instructor notes.

After completing this course, students will know how to:

- Stay current with the activities of colleagues on social networks, such as SharePoint; subscribe to RSS news feeds; and read articles within a feed.
- Manage the mailbox by deleting old and unneeded messages, deleting the contents of automatic folders, and compacting the mailbox; and archive messages to local files and the archive mailbox.
- Create, forward, and customize notes; create automatic and manual Journal entries; and open and modify Journal entries.
- Share access to their calendar with others; use their SharePoint calendar and contacts in Outlook; share contacts with others; and export contacts.
- Send many personalized e-mail messages by using mail merge; create e-mail templates; and send messages based on those templates.

Skills inventory

Use the following form to gauge students' skill levels entering the class (students have copies in the introductions of their student manuals). For each skill listed, have students rate their familiarity from 1 to 5, with 5 being the most familiar. Emphasize that this isn't a test. Rather, it's intended to provide students with an idea of where they're starting from at the beginning of class. If a student is wholly unfamiliar with all the skills, he or she might not be ready for the class. A student who seems to understand all of the skills, on the other hand, might need to move on to the next course in the series.

Skill	1	2	3	4	5
Connecting Outlook to your social network account					
Connecting to a colleague					
Viewing social network activity in the People Pane					
Subscribing to RSS feeds					
Cleaning up your Inbox and automatic folders					
Archiving mail messages manually and automatically					
Restoring archived messages					
Archiving messages to your Exchange archive mailbox					
Creating and working with notes					
Creating Journal entries automatically and manually					
Opening and modifying a Journal entry					
Sharing your calendar and contacts					
Granting and removing folder sharing permissions					
Delegating access to your calendar and contacts					
Accessing your SharePoint calendar in Outlook					
Accessing SharePoint contacts within Outlook					
Creating templates and sending messages that use templates					
Sending many e-mail messages by using mail merge					

Topic C: Classroom setup

All our courses assume that each student has a personal computer to use during the class. Our hands-on approach to learning requires that they do. This topic gives information on how to set up the classroom to teach this course.

In our experience, you cannot install Exchange, SQL Server, and SharePoint on a single server. Doing so might not be completely impossible, but such a setup will be difficult and is not documented here.

This course requires two Windows Server 2008 64-bit Edition servers: one that serves as your domain controller and runs the Exchange Server software; and one that runs Windows SharePoint Services and its required components. If you use a computer with sufficient resources, you can use server virtualization software (Hyper-V, VirtualBox, XenServer, VMWare, and so forth) to run two virtual servers on a single physical computer.

Due to the complexity and time required to complete the server setup, we recommend that you do one of the following:

- Set up the servers, using a virtualization system. After the setup is complete, use your virtualization system's tools to save "snapshots" of the working servers.

- Use a tool such as Acronis TrueImage, Norton Ghost, or CloneZilla to save "images" of your working servers after you have completed the setup.

Either of these methods will enable you to revert to those snapshots or images after class, rather than having to set up the entire environment again.

Hardware requirements

Each classroom server should have:

- A keyboard and a mouse
- At least 1.4 GHz 64-bit processor (2 GHz or faster recommended)
- At least 2 GB RAM (4 GB or greater recommended)
- At least 100 GB hard drive
- A DVD-ROM drive
- SVGA monitor at 1024×768 resolution

The instructor computer and each student computer should have:

- A keyboard and a mouse
- At least 1 GHz 32-bit or 64-bit processor
- At least 1 GB RAM
- At least 50 GB hard drive with at least 15 GB of available space
- A DVD-ROM drive
- A graphics card that supports DirectX 9 graphics with:
  - WDDM driver
  - 128 MB of graphics memory (minimum)
  - Pixel Shader 2.0 in hardware
  - 32 bits per pixel
- SVGA monitor

Software requirements

You will need the following software:

- Windows Server 2008 Standard 64-bit Edition with Service Pack 2
- Microsoft Exchange Server 2010 Standard Edition
- Microsoft SharePoint 2010
- Microsoft SQL Server 2008 R2
- Windows 7 Professional
- Microsoft Outlook 2010, which is included with the Microsoft Office 2010 Home and Business, Standard, Professional, and Professional Plus editions

Network requirements

The following network components and connectivity are also required for this course:

- Internet access, for the following purposes:
  - Downloading the latest critical updates and service packs from www.windowsupdate.com
  - Completing activities throughout the course
  - Downloading the Student Data files from www.axzopress.com (if necessary)
- A static IPv4 address for each of the classroom servers on the same subnet as the student and instructor computers. You will need a DHCP server available on that subnet and a pool of addresses sufficient for the instructor and student computers.

Classroom setup instructions

Classroom server installation

Before you teach this course, you will need to perform the following steps on *both* of the classroom servers.

1 Install Windows Server 2008 Standard, using the following information.
   a Don't go online to get the latest updates for installation.
   b Select the appropriate language, time and currency format, and keyboard or input method.
   c Select Windows Server 2008 Standard (Full Installation).
   d Accept the license agreement.
   e Choose a custom installation. Create at least a 40 GB partition and format it as NTFS.
   f When prompted, enter and confirm a password of **!pass1234** for the Administrator account.
   g When prompted, select Work as your network location.
2 If necessary, change your display settings to at least 1024×768.

3 Configure the server, using the Initial Configuration Tasks window.

    a Set the correct time zone and time.

    b Configure networking for the Local Area Connection:

        – If necessary, install a driver for the network adapter.

        – Specify the appropriate static IPv4 addressing parameters, including an IP address, subnet mask, and default gateway address, for your classroom network.

    c On the computer that will be the Exchange server, name the computer **winserver**. On the computer that will be the SharePoint server, name the computer **spserver**. Restart when prompted.

    d Install the Web Server (IIS) role.

        i In the Initial Configuration Tasks window, under Customize This Server, click Add roles. Click Next.

        ii Select Web Server (IIS) and click Next.

        iii Select all role services. Click Next.

        iv If prompted, install any required role services and features.

        v Click Install.

        vi When the installation is complete, close the Initial Configuration Tasks window.

4 Turn off Internet Explorer Enhanced Security Configuration.

    a In Server Manager, select the Server Manager console root.

    b Under Security Information, click Configure IE ESC.

    c Under Administrators, select Off. Under Users, select Off. Click OK.

    d Leave Server Manager open.

5 If your copy of Windows Server 2008 Standard Edition didn't include Service Pack 2, install it now. You can do this from Microsoft's Windows Update site. (Use caution when allowing Windows Update to install any files newer than SP2, as this course wasn't keytested using newer patches.)

Exchange Server 2010 installation

Perform the following steps on the computer that will be your Exchange server.

1 Install the Active Directory Domain Services role.

    a In Server Manager, under Roles Summary, click Add roles. Click Next.

    b Select Active Directory Domain Services, and click Next twice. Click Install.

    c Click Start, choose Run, and enter **dcpromo**. Click Next twice.

    d Select "Create a new domain in a new forest" and click Next.

    e In the FQDN text box, type **outlanderspices.com**, and click Next.

    f In the Forest functional level list, select Windows Server 2008. Click Next.

    g Verify that DNS server is selected, and click Next. Click Yes.

    h Click Next to accept the default locations for the database folder, the log files folder, and the SYSVOL folder.

    i Enter and confirm **!pass1234** as the restore-mode administrator password. Click Next twice.

    j Check "Reboot on completion."

2   Log on as the domain administrator. In the Initial Configuration Tasks window, check "Do not show this window at logon" and click Close.

3   Insert the Exchange Server DVD into your server's drive.

4   In the AutoPlay dialog box, click Run Setup.exe.

5   Click "Step 1: Install .NET Framework 3.5 SP1" and follow these steps to install the .NET framework:

   a   Internet Explorer opens and a page on the Microsoft downloads site is loaded. Click Download.

   b   Click Run to download and run the .NET framework installation file.

   c   Click Run again to install the .NET framework.

   d   Close all open windows except for Exchange Server.

6   Click "Step 2: Install Windows PowerShell v2" and follow these steps to install the PowerShell component:

   a   Internet Explorer opens and a page on the Microsoft support site is loaded. Scroll about halfway down the page to locate the "Windows Management Framework Core (WinRM 2.0 and Windows PowerShell 2.0)" heading.

   b   Download the 64-bit Windows server package by clicking "Download the Windows Management Framework Core for Windows Server 2008 x64 Edition package now."

   c   Run and install the Windows Management Framework Core package.

   d   Click Restart Now.

7   Log on as Administrator and then close Server Manager.

8   Use Windows PowerShell to install the required server components:

   a   Click Start and choose All Programs, Administrative Tools, Windows PowerShell Modules. If prompted for administrator credentials, enter **Administrator** as the user name and **!pass1234** as the password.

   b   Type
```
ServerManagerCmd -ip d:\scripts\Exchange-Typical.xml
```
and press Enter. The script will install various required components.

   c   When returned to the prompt, close Windows PowerShell Modules (either click the X, or type `exit` and press Enter).

   d   Restart your server. (Click Start. Beside the Shutdown and Lock buttons, click the triangle button and choose Restart. From the Option list, select Application Installation (Planned). Click OK.)

9   Log on as Administrator and then close Server Manager.

10 Use the Windows PowerShell to set the NetTcpPortSharing service to start automatically:

   a   Click Start and choose Windows PowerShell.

   b   At the prompt, type
```
Set-Service NetTcpPortSharing -StartupType Automatic
```
and press Enter.

   c   Type `exit` and press Enter.

11 Install the 2007 Office System Converter: Microsoft Filter Pack by following these steps:

    a Open Internet Explorer. In the Address bar, enter **http://go.microsoft.com/fwlink/?LinkID=123380**

    b Scroll to the bottom of the page. Next to FilterPackx64.exe, click Download.

    c Click Run, and then click Run again. Click Next.

    d Check "I accept the terms in the License Agreement" and click Next.

    e Click OK. Close Internet Explorer.

12 Eject and then insert the Exchange DVD. In the AutoPlay dialog box, click Run Setup.exe.

13 Click "Step 3: Choose Exchange Language option." Then click "Install only languages from the DVD."

14 Click "Step 4: Install Microsoft Exchange," click Next, and follow these steps to install Exchange:

    a Select "I accept the terms in the license agreement" and click Next.

    b With No selected in the Error Reporting options, click Next.

    c With Typical Exchange Server Installation selected, click Next.

    d In the "Specify the name for this Exchange organization" box, enter **Outlander Spices** and click Next.

    e On the Client Settings page, select No (if necessary) and click Next.

    f Click Next (do not check "The Client Access Server role will be Internet-facing").

    g Select "I don't wish to join the program at this time" and click Next.

    h On the Readiness Checks page, you will likely receive a warning message about not installing Exchange 2007 server roles. That is fine. If you receive any failure messages, correct the problems by following the on-screen instructions. You can leave this page of the wizard open and click Retry after correcting problems.

    i Click Install. The Progress page will display the installation progress. Depending on the speed of your server, the installation could take as long as an hour to finish.

    j Click Finish.

    k Close the Exchange Management Console.

15 Click "Step 5: Get critical updates for Microsoft Exchange" and follow these steps to install the updates:

    a If necessary, click "I agree to the Terms of Use for Microsoft Update."

    b Click Next.

    c Select Use Recommended Settings, and click Install.

    d If updates are found, install them, following the on-screen instructions. Restart if prompted.

16 Click Close. Remove the DVD from your drive.

Creating user accounts for students

You will need to create a user account for yourself and for each student in class. Name your account **Instructor**, and name each student account **Student##** where ## is a unique number you assign to each account.

During class, students will work in pairs to complete some activities. If you have an odd number of students, you can work with one of the students as his or her partner. If you have an even number of students, you will need a partner user account (though not a computer) to key through the partnered activities. If necessary, create a **Student999** account to use as your partner in a class with an even number of students.

1 Create an account for each student/instructor, as described, by following these steps:

     a In Server Manager, expand Roles, Active Directory Domain Services, Active Directory Users and Computers, and the outlanderspices.com domain.

     b In the Users folder, right-click a blank space and choose New, User.

     c Leave the First Name and Initials fields blank. In the Last Name and Logon Name boxes, enter the account name (for example, **Instructor** or **Student##**).

     d Click Next.

     e Enter and confirm a password of **!pass1234**. Uncheck "User must change password at next logon." Check "User cannot change password" and "Password never expires."

     f Click Next. Click Finish.

2 Create a security group and add the user accounts you just created to it by following these steps:

     a In Active Directory Users and Computers, right-click the Users folder and choose New, Group.

     b In the Group name box, enter **SP Users**. Confirm that Global is selected for the scope and that Security is selected for the type. Click OK.

     c Select all of the user accounts you created, including the Instructor. (Use Shift+click or Ctrl+click to select multiple accounts.)

     d Right-click any of the selected accounts and choose "Add to a group."

     e In the object names box, enter **SP Users**. Click Check Names. Click OK twice.

3 Close Active Directory Users and Computers.

4 Close Server Manager.

Creating mailboxes

Mailbox creation in Exchange Server 2010 is not managed through Active Directory, as was done with previous versions of the software. To create mailboxes, you must use an Exchange-specific tool.

1 On the Exchange server, click Start and choose All Programs, Microsoft Exchange Server 2010, Exchange Management Console.

2 Expand Microsoft Exchange on-Premises (winserver.outlanderspices.com).

3 Select Recipient Configuration.

4 In the middle pane, right-click and choose New Mailbox.

5 With User Mailbox selected, click Next.

6 Select Existing users. Click Add.

7 Select all of the accounts you added (use Ctrl+click or Shift+click to select them all) and click OK. Click Next.

8 Click Next. Click New to create a mailbox for each user you selected.

9 Click Finish.

10 Select all of the student mailboxes plus the Instructor mailbox. In the Actions pane, click Enable Archive. Click Yes to acknowledge the licensing requirements.

11 Close the Exchange Management Console.

SharePoint 2010 installation

Perform the following steps on the computer that will be your SharePoint server.

1 Join the classroom domain by following these steps:

    a Configure the SharePoint server to use the Exchange/domain-controller server as its DNS server, as follows:

        i In Server Manager, click View Network Connections.

        ii Right-click your network connection and choose Properties.

        iii Double-click Internet Protocol Version 4 (TCP/IPv4).

        iv If necessary, select "Use the following DNS server addresses." Then, in the Preferred DNS server boxes, enter your Exchange server's IP address. You can enter another DNS server's address in the Alternate DNS server boxes, if appropriate for your network.

        v Click OK twice. Close the Network Connections window.

    b In Server Manager, click Change System Properties.

    c Click Change.

    d Beneath Member of, select Domain and enter **outlanderspices.com**. Click OK.

    e When prompted for credentials, enter the domain administrator's user name and password. If you followed the setup notes described previously, the credentials should be Administrator and !pass1234.

    f Click OK. Then click OK again, click Close, and click Restart Now.

2 Log on as the domain administrator. In the Initial Configuration Tasks window, check "Do not show this window at logon" and click Close.

3 Configure the Windows Firewall to pass traffic on ports 1433 and 1434 as follows:

    a Click Start and type **Firewall**. Then click Windows Firewall with Advanced Security.

    b Click Inbound Rules.

    c Click New Rule to open the New Inbound Rule Wizard.

    d Select Port and click Next.

    e Confirm that TCP is selected. In the Specific local ports box, enter **1433, 1434**. Click Next.

    f Confirm that "Allow the connection" is selected and click Next.

    g Click Next to permit the connection at the domain, private, and public levels.

    h In the Name box, enter **SQL Server**. Click Finish.

    i Close Windows Firewall with Advanced Security.

4   Install SQL Server 2008 R2 by following these steps:

  a   Insert the SQL Server 2008 R2 DVD into your server's drive. In the AutoPlay dialog box, click Run Setup.exe.

  b   If prompted that the .NET Framework and other components are required, click OK and follow the prompts to install these components. When the .NET installation is complete, click Exit.

  c   Click Installation. Then click "New installation or add features to an existing installation."

  d   On the Setup Support Rules page, click OK.

  e   If you have a product key available, select "Enter the product key" and then enter the key. Otherwise, select "Specify a free edition" and select Evaluation from the list. Click Next.

  f   Accept the software license terms and click Next.

  g   Click Install.

  h   Correct any problems identified on the Setup Support Rules page of the wizard (ignore the Windows Firewall warning). Click Next.

  i   Select All Features With Defaults. Click Next five times to advance to the Server Configuration page of the wizard.

  j   On the Server Configuration, Service Accounts page, for SQL Server Agent, point to the Account Name cell, and when the drop-down list appears, select NT AUTHORITY\SYSTEM. Configure the SQL Server Analysis Services to also use the NTAUTHORITY\SYSTEM account. Click Next.

  k   Click Next to accept the default Windows authentication mode option.

  l   On the Analysis Services Configuration page, click Add Current User and click Next.

  m   Select "Install the SharePoint integrated mode default configuration" and click Next.

  n   Click Next twice; then click Install. Depending on the speed of your computer, installing the software will likely take considerable time.

  o   Click Close and then close the SQL Server Installation Center to finish the installation.

  p   Remove the DVD from the drive.

5   Install the software prerequisites for SharePoint 2010 by following these steps:

  a   Insert the SharePoint 2010 DVD into your server's drive.

  b   In the AutoPlay dialog box, click Run splash.hta.

  c   Click "Install software prerequisites."

  d   Click Next. Accept the license agreement and click Next again.

  e   Click Finish.

  f   If prompted to restart your server, do so and then log back on as the domain administrator.

6 Install SharePoint 2010 by following these steps:

   a Eject and then insert the SharePoint 2010 DVD into your server's drive. Run splash.hta.

   b Click Install SharePoint Server.

   c Enter your SharePoint product key and click Continue.

   d Accept the license terms and click Continue.

   e Click Server Farm to install the software in a custom configuration on a single server.

   f Select Complete and click Install Now.

   g At the end of the installation wizard, with "Run the SharePoint Products Configuration Wizard now" checked, click Close.

These SharePoint setup steps do not represent Microsoft's "best practice" recommendations for a production environment. They are meant to create a usable environment suitable for the classroom.

7 Use the SharePoint Products Configuration Wizard to configure your SharePoint server as follows:

   a Click Next. You're prompted that some services will be started or reset during configuration. Click Yes.

   b Select "Create a new server farm" and click Next.

   c In the Database server box, enter **SPServer**. Leave the database name set to SharePoint_Config. Enter **Outlanderspices\Administrator** in the Username box, and enter **!pass1234** in the password box. Click Next.

   d In the Passphrase and Confirm passphrase boxes, enter **!pass1234** and click Next.

   e When prompted for a port and security settings, click Next to accept the default settings.

   f Click Next. The wizard will spend a significant amount of time configuring SharePoint and its components. When it's done, click Finish.

   g Internet Explorer opens. If you're prompted to turn on the Phishing Filter during these steps, select "Turn on automatic Phishing Filter" and click OK.

   h When prompted to sign up for the Customer Experience Improvement Program, select "No, I don't wish to participate" and click OK.

   i Click "Start the wizard" to open the server farm configuration wizard.

   j Select "Use existing managed account" and confirm that Outlanderspices\Administrator is selected. Click Next. The server farm configuration wizard may take a considerable amount of time to finish. Leave the browser window open; do not refresh the page or navigate away during this time.

   k In the Title box, enter **Outlander Spices Intranet**. In the Template Selection area, confirm that Team Site is selected. Click OK.

   l Click Finish.

8   Configure Active Directory synchronization as follows:

a   In SharePoint Central Administration, click Application Management.

b   Click "Manage Services on server."

c   Next to User Profile Synchronization Service, click Start.

d   Enter **!pass1234** in the Password and Confirm password boxes. Click OK.

e   It will take a considerable amount of time, perhaps 30 minutes, for the service to start. You can refresh the page to check its progress.

f   Once the service is listed as started, reset IIS by following these steps:

   i   Click Start and choose Command Prompt

   ii   Type `iisreset` and press Enter.

   iii   Type `exit` and press Enter.

g   Click Application Management. Then click Manage Service Applications. Scroll down. In the list, click the blue (not indented) User Profile Service Application link.

h   Click Configure Synchronization Connections.

If you get a "MOSS MA not found" error, use the Services console to start the two Forefront Identity Manager services. Then try again.

i   Click Create a New Connection. Enter the following information:

   –   Connection Name: **AD Connection**

   –   Forest name: **Outlanderspices**

   –   Account name: **Outlanderspices\Administrator**

   –   Password and Confirm password: **!pass1234**

   Click Populate Containers. Expand the Outlanderspices container. Check Users and then click OK.

j   Click Application Management and then click Manage Service Applications. Scroll down. In the list, click the blue (not indented) User Profile Service Application link.

k   In the People section, click Manage User Properties. In the list, locate Picture and point to it. When the drop-down list appears, select Edit.

l   Scroll down to the Display Settings section. Make sure all three options in this section are checked.

m   In the Add New Mapping section, set the Source Data Connection to AD Connection. From the Attribute list, select thumbnailPhoto. In the Direction list, select Export. Click Add. Click OK.

n   Click Application Management and then click Manage Service Applications. Scroll down. In the list, click the blue (not indented) User Profile Service Application link.

o   Click Start Profile Synchronization.

p   Confirm that Start Incremental Synchronization is selected and click OK. You will be returned to the Manage Profile Service: User Profile Service Application page. The status indicator might not show progress on the synchronization. You can wait a few minutes and refresh the page. Eventually you should see the word Synchronizing in the right column under Profile Synchronization Settings. Refresh the page occasionally until the status is "Idle" again.

q Confirm that user profiles were imported, as follows: Click Manage User Profiles. In the Find profiles box, enter **student** and click Find. If prompted to turn on AutoComplete, click Yes.

You should see a list of all of the student accounts you created earlier in the setup steps. If you don't, return to the Manage Profile Service: User Profile Service Application page and wait until the process finishes.

9 Configure user permissions to access the SharePoint team site as follows:

a Click Application Management and then click Manage Web Applications.

b Click to select SharePoint – 80 and click User Policy.

c Click Add Users. Click Next. In the Users box, enter **SP Users**. Click the Check Names button. Check Full Control. Click Finish. Click OK.

d In the upper-right corner, from the System Account menu, choose My Site.

e From the Site Actions menu, choose Site Permissions.

f Check "NT Authority\authenticated users" and click Edit User Permissions.

g Check Design and Contribute, and click OK.

10 Enable the Activity Feed Timer Job as follows:

a Click Start and choose All Programs, Microsoft SharePoint 2010 Products, SharePoint 2010 Central Administration.

b Click Monitoring. Click "Review job definitions."

c In the list, locate User Profile Service Application – Activity Feed Job and click it. (It is near the end of the list.)

d In the Recurring Schedule section, select Minutes, and enter 1 in the box.

e Click Enable.

11 Enable outgoing SMTP support for SharePoint by configuring the Exchange server as follows:

a On the Exchange server, log on and open the Exchange Management Console.

b Expand Server Configuration and select Hub Transport.

c In the right pane, click New Receive Connector.

d Enter **SharePoint Outgoing Mail** in the Name box. Make sure Custom is selected in the list box, and click Next.

e Click Next to accept the default local network settings.

f Click Edit. In the starting range box, enter the IP address of your SharePoint server; then click OK. Click Next.

g Click New; then click Finish to close the dialog box.

h Double-click the new connector to open its Properties dialog box. Click the Permission Groups tab. Check Anonymous users and click OK.

i Close the Exchange Management Console and log off.

12 Enable outgoing SMTP support for SharePoint by configuring the SharePoint server as follows:

    a On the SharePoint server, open the Central Administration site.

    b Click System Settings.

    c Click "Configure outgoing e-mail settings."

    d Enter these settings:

        – Outbound SMTP server: **winserver** (your Exchange server's name)

        – From address: **administrator@outlanderspices.com**

        – Reply-to address: **administrator@outlanderspices.com**

    e Click OK.

13 Close all windows and log off.

Setting up the instructor and student computers

You will need to perform the following steps to set up the instructor computer and each student computer:

1 Install Windows 7 on an NTFS partition according to the software manufacturer's instructions, following these additional detail steps:

    a If prompted, click the button specifying to go online and get the latest updates.

    b In the Set Up Windows dialog box, in the "Type a user name" box, type **Admin**.

    c In the "Type a computer name" box, type **Computer##** to match the user account names you created for the students. Use **Instructor** for your computer's name.

    d Click Next. In the Type a password box, type **!pass**. In the Password Hint box, type **Exclamation abbreviation**.

    e Click Next. Enter your Windows 7 product key, and click Next.

    f On the "Help protect your computer and improve Windows automatically" page, click "Use recommended settings."

    g Click Next. From the Time zone list, select your time zone, and verify the accuracy of the current time. Edit the time if necessary.

    h Click Next. On the Windows networking page, select Work. Windows completes the setup and displays the desktop.

2 Configure each computer to use your classroom server as the DNS server. To do so:

    a In the notification area of the taskbar, right-click the Network icon and choose Open Network and Sharing Center.

    b In the "View your active networks" section, beside Connections, click Local Area Connection.

    c Click Properties.

    d Select Internet Protocol Version 4 (TCP/IPv4) and click Properties.

    e Select "Use the following DNS server addresses." In the Preferred DNS server boxes, enter your classroom server's IP address.

    f Click OK, click Close twice, and close the Network and Sharing Center.

3 On each computer, join the classroom domain by following these steps:

  a Click Start. Right-click Computer and choose Properties.

  b In the "Computer name, domain, and workgroup settings" section, click Change Settings.

  c Click Change.

  d Beneath Member of, select Domain and enter **outlanderspices.com**. Click OK.

  e When prompted for credentials, enter the domain administrator's user name and password. If you followed the setup notes described previously, the credentials should be Administrator and !pass1234.

  f Click OK. Then click OK again, click Close, and click Restart Now.

4 From the student and instructor computers, log onto the domain:

  a Click Switch User.

  b Click Other User.

  c Enter the user name associated with the computer (for example, enter Student01 on Computer01).

  d Enter **!pass1234** as the password and click the logon arrow.

5 Install Microsoft Office 2010 according to the software manufacturer's instructions, as follows:

  a When prompted for the CD key, enter the code included with your software. Accept the license agreement.

  b Click Customize.

  c If necessary, click the Installation Options tab.

  d For Microsoft Excel, Microsoft OneNote, Microsoft Outlook, Microsoft Word, Office Shared Features, and Office Tools, click the down-arrow and select "Run all from My Computer."

  e For Microsoft SharePoint Workspace, select "Run from My Computer."

  f Set all other components (those not specified in steps 5d and 5e) to Not Available.

  g Click Install Now.

  h On the last screen of the Office 2010 installer, click Continue Online. Internet Explorer displays the Office Online Web site, and the installer window closes.

  i If you are prompted to set up Windows Internet Explorer 8: Click Next, select Yes, turn on Suggested Sites, click Next, select "Use express settings," and click Finish. Close the Welcome to Internet Explorer 8 tab.

  j On the Welcome to Microsoft Office 2010 Web page, below Check for updates, click Check now.

  k Windows Update opens. Click "Check for updates." If updates are found, click Install updates. Follow the on-screen prompts to download and install the updates.

  l Close Windows Update and Internet Explorer.

6 On each computer, configure Outlook to connect to the corresponding student account mailbox. For example, on Computer01, connect Outlook to the Student01 mailbox.

   a Click Start and choose All Programs, Microsoft Office, Microsoft Outlook 2010.

   b Click Next. Click Next again.

   c Account information should be acquired automatically from the domain. Click Next.

   d When prompted with a Security Alert about a problem with the site's security, follow these steps to install the certificate on the student computer:

      i   Click View Certificate.

      ii   Click Install Certificate. Click Next twice.

      iii Click Finish. Click Yes.

      iv   Click OK twice.

      v   Click Yes to close the Security Alert dialog box.

   e Click Finish.

   f In the User Name dialog box, enter a name and initials for the student. For example, in the Name box, enter **Student Number ##**, and in the Initials box, enter **SN##**, where ## is the user's account number. Click OK.

   g In the Help Protect and Improve Microsoft Office section, select Use Recommended Settings. Click OK.

   h In the User Account Control dialog box, enter **Administrator** and **!pass1234** and click Yes.

   i Close Microsoft Outlook.

7 On each computer, edit the Registry as follows:

   a Click Start. In the search box, type **regedit** and press Enter.

   b Navigate to **HKEY_CURRENT_USER\Software\Microsoft\Office\Outlook\SocialConnector**.

   c If the ActivitySyncInterval value is defined, double-click it to open it for editing.

      If the ActivitySyncInterval value is not defined, right-click a blank area in the right pane and choose New, DWORD (32-bit) Value. Type **ActivitySyncInterval** and press Enter. Then double-click the new value to open it for editing.

   d Select Decimal and enter **1** in the Value data box.

   e Click OK.

   f Close the Registry Editor.

8 If you have the data disc that came with this manual, locate the Student Data folder on it and copy it to the desktop of each student computer.

If you don't have the data disc, you can download the Student Data files for the course:

 a Connect to www.axzopress.com.

 b Under Downloads, click Instructor-Led Training.

 c Browse the subject categories to locate your course. Then click the course title to display a list of available downloads. (You can also access these downloads through our Catalog listings.)

 d Click the link(s) for downloading the Student Data files. You can download the files directly to student machines or to a central location on your own network.

 e Create a folder named Student Data on the desktop of each student computer.

 f Double-click the downloaded zip file(s) and drag the contents into the Student Data folder.

9 From the instructor's computer, send two e-mail messages to each student. Make sure to send copies of the messages to the Instructor account as well. For the first message, use the subject "Welcome to Outlook 2010" and enter a message of your choice in the Message area. For the second message, use "Your second message" as the subject and enter a message of your choice.

CertBlaster software

CertBlaster pre- and post-assessment software is available for this course. To download and install this free software, students should complete the following steps:

1 Go to www.axzopress.com.

2 Under Downloads, click CertBlaster.

3 Click the link for Outlook 2010.

4 Save the .EXE file to a folder on your hard drive. (**Note:** If you skip this step, the CertBlaster software will not install correctly.)

5 Click Start and choose Run.

6 Click Browse and navigate to the folder that contains the .EXE file.

7 Select the .EXE file and click Open.

8 Click OK and follow the on-screen instructions. When prompted for the password, enter **c_ol2010**.

Topic D: Support

Your success is our primary concern. If you need help setting up this class or teaching a particular unit, topic, or activity, please don't hesitate to get in touch with us.

Contacting us

Please contact us through our Web site, www.axzopress.com. You will need to provide the name of the course, and be as specific as possible about the kind of help you need.

Instructor's tools

Our Web site provides several instructor's tools for each course, including course outlines and answers to frequently asked questions. To download these files, go to www.axzopress.com. Then, under Downloads, click Instructor-Led Training and browse our subject categories.

Unit 1

Collaboration

Unit time: 45 minutes

Complete this unit, and you'll know how to:

A Connect with SharePoint colleagues by using the Outlook Social Connector.

B Gather news and information from RSS feeds.

Topic A: Connecting with colleagues via Outlook Social Connectors

This topic covers the following Microsoft Office Specialist exam objective for Outlook 2010.

#	Objective
1.3	**Arrange the content pane**
	1.3.4 Use the People Pane

Outlook Social Connectors

Explanation

Outlook 2010 adds social networking support through *Outlook Social Connectors*. An OSC is like a pipeline between Outlook and a social network, such as Facebook, SharePoint, or LinkedIn. With an OSC enabled, the People Pane displays status updates, profile changes, and other social network activity.

Objective 1.3.4

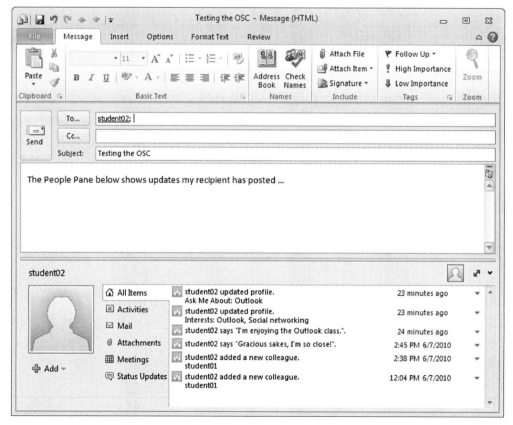

Exhibit 1-1: Status updates on a social network are displayed in the People Pane

OSCs are supported by Office Home and Business, Office Professional Plus, and Office Pro. At the time of this writing, connectors for Facebook, Windows SharePoint Server, and Windows Live Messenger were available from Microsoft. Third-party connectors were available for LinkedIn, MySpace, and SocialWok. Others were in development.

You can visit www.microsoft.com/office/2010/en/socialconnector/default.aspx to get more information about the available OSCs. Not all connectors will be listed on that page. If you search the Internet, you will likely find other OSCs from smaller social networking providers.

You must specify whether to install the SharePoint OSC when installing Outlook. Depending on the installation choices made, the SharePoint OSC might not be available to you. Other OSCs must be installed by following the instructions provided by their publishers. If an OSC is installed, the People Pane will contain buttons you can use to add connections to colleagues on the associated social network.

Do it!

A-1: Examining the available OSCs

Here's how	Here's why
1 Open Internet Explorer	
2 If prompted to set up Internet Explorer, do the following: Click **Next**, select **No, don't turn on**, click **Next**, select **Use express settings**, and click **Finish** Close the Welcome to Internet Explorer 8 tab	
3 Visit **http://tinyurl.com/24dkhdt**	Or visit http://office.microsoft.com/en-us/outlook/social-connector-for-microsoft-outlook-HA101794273.aspx.
4 Observe the list of available OSCs	At the time of this writing, this Microsoft page listed the available connectors, which included LinkedIn and MySpace. Others were listed as "coming soon."
5 Visit **www.xobni.com**	Xobni offers an Outlook add-in that performs similar functions as the Outlook Social Connector. Other add-ins that perform similar functions include Outsync, Fblook, TwInbox, and Yammer.

These products are not OSCs, but add-ins that link Outlook with a social network by using custom techniques.

SharePoint

Explanation

SharePoint is a collaboration tool published by Microsoft. Using SharePoint, companies and teams can share documents, coordinate schedules, and manage lists of information, such as contact lists, lists of links, and so forth. SharePoint can be used to create a private and secure in-house social network among employees. SharePoint can also be used on the Internet to extend this private collaboration system to partners and suppliers.

SharePoint is highly customizable. In its "team site" configuration, each employee has his or her own Web site space, or *My Site* as it's called in SharePoint terminology. Users can log onto their My Sites to post news and notes, upload documents, manage contact lists, and more. Users can share this information with colleagues. Each user can also maintain a profile, which lists his or her contact information, skills, interests, and more.

The first time you log on, SharePoint creates your My Site and performs various behind-the-scenes configuration steps. This setup process can take a few minutes and must be completed before you can view or post updates to your My Site.

SharePoint 2010 uses a mix of buttons, drop-down menus, and tabs to provide the navigation links you need to work with your My Site space. When present, tabs in SharePoint work just like tabs in any of the other Office 2010 applications.

Do it!

A-2: Creating your SharePoint profile

Here's how	Here's why
1 In Internet Explorer, visit **http://spserver/my/**	To visit the classroom SharePoint server. You are automatically logged onto your "My Site" Web page.
2 If prompted to log on, enter **outlanderspices\student##** for the user name and **!pass1234** for the password	
3 Click **My Content**	(In the top-left corner of the page.) SharePoint sets up your personal site. It will take a few minutes for the process to finish.
4 On the Internet Explorer toolbar, click where indicated	
Choose **Add or change home page…**	
Select **Use this web page as your only home page**	
Click **Yes**	To set the current page as your start (home) page.

OSC configuration

Explanation

Connecting to a person on a social network is a two-step process. First, you must configure your overall connection to the social network. Second, you connect to the individual.

Objective 1.3.4

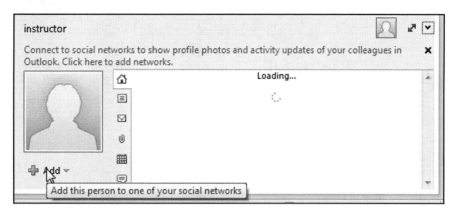

Exhibit 1-2: The Add button in the People Pane

To connect to a social network:

1 In the People Pane, click the Add button, as shown in Exhibit 1-2, and choose "on another social network."

2 Click Next.

3 Click the social network you want to connect to, such as My Site (for a SharePoint network).

4 Enter the information, including logon credentials, required by the social network.

For example, for SharePoint, enter the URL for your SharePoint My Site page, your SharePoint user name (which is probably your domain user account), and your password. Check "Remember my password" unless you want to log onto the network each time you open Outlook.

5 Click Connect.

6 Click Finish and then click Close.

Do it!

Objective 1.3.4

A-3: Connecting Outlook to your SharePoint profile

Here's how	Here's why
1 Open Outlook	Your instructor should have sent you at least two e-mail messages.
2 In the People Pane, click ⌃	To expand the People Pane.
3 Below the picture placeholder, click **Add**	To begin the process of connecting to a social network.
4 Click **Next**	
5 Click **My Site**	
6 Enter the following information: URL Address: **http://spserver/my/** User name: **outlanderspices\student##** Password: **!pass1234**	
7 Click **Connect**	
8 Click **Finish**	
9 Click **Close**	

Connecting to colleagues

Once you have connected to your account on the social network, you must connect with an individual on that network in order to see his or her updates in the People Pane. To do so:

1   Exchange an e-mail message with the individual with whom you want to connect. You must have received a message from that person in order to connect to him or her. In order for that person to connect to you, you must have sent him or her an e-mail message.

2   In the Folder Contents list, select an e-mail message from the person with whom you want to connect.

3   In the People Pane, click the "Add this person to one of your social networks" button and choose the command appropriate to your social network. For example, for SharePoint, choose "on My Site."

4   Click Continue. Depending on the social network, additional steps might be required. For example, the person you're connecting to might need to approve the connection.

A-4:   Using the People Pane to connect to a colleague

Here's how	Here's why
1 Send an e-mail message to your partner	You can use any subject and message.
2 When your partner's message arrives, click **Add**, as shown	
Choose **on My Site**	
3 Click **Continue**	
	A new icon indicates that you have connected with your partner. It can take up to an hour for status updates to begin showing up in the People Pane. For now, that pane likely says that there are no items to show.

Monitoring social network activities

Explanation

SharePoint's My Site system enables you to post status updates, share notes with colleagues, create a profile that describes you, and share documents. Other social networks offer similar features for interacting with colleagues.

Objective 1.3.4

You will see notices in the People Pane when your colleagues update their My Site content. Not every type of update or change they make will be displayed in the People Pane. Status updates and note postings are two such activities that will be displayed in the pane.

Depending on the configuration options set by your SharePoint administrator, status updates can take an hour or more to show up in Outlook. Other networks, such as LinkedIn, will have different update intervals. If you need more timely updates, you'll be better off using the social network's specific tools or Web sites.

Do it!

Objective 1.3.4

A-5: Monitoring your colleague's status

The files for this activity are in Student Data folder **Unit 1\Topic A**.

Here's how	Here's why
1 Switch to Internet Explorer	Your My Site page should be open.
2 Click **My Profile**	
3 Click where indicated, and type a brief status message Press ↵ ENTER	 For example, type "I'm enjoying the Outlook class."
4 Click **Edit My Profile**	
5 Click **Choose Picture**	You will add a picture to your profile.
Click **Browse**	
Navigate to the current topic folder	Student Data folder Unit 1\Topic A.
Select a picture and click **Open**	
Click **OK**	To add the picture.
6 Scroll down	
In the Interests box, enter **Outlook; Social networking**	
7 Click **Save and Close**	(At the bottom of the page.) To save your profile.
8 Switch to Outlook	
9 Compose a message to your partner	
10 If necessary, expand the People Pane	It can take up to an hour for status updates to begin showing up in the People Pane. For now, that pane likely shows only the e-mail message you received from your partner. You might see a message stating that your partner has added you as a colleague.
11 Close the message	Without sending it.

Contact information

Explanation

Outlook automatically saves contact information for the colleagues you connect to on a social network. When you're working with SharePoint, such contacts are added to a My Sites folder, which you can view by clicking the Folder List button in the Navigation pane. The same folder is available if you open the Contacts folder.

Outlook does not detect or manage duplicates. For example, let's say you have a contact entry for a colleague in your address book. Then you connect with her via the OSC. You will then have two entries for her—one in your main Contacts list and one in the My Sites contacts list.

Do it!

A-6: Viewing My Site contacts

Here's how	Here's why
1 In the Navigation pane, click the Folder List button, as shown	
2 In the list of folders, click **My Site**	This folder contains contacts with whom you've connected via the SharePoint social connector. Your partner's card should be listed.
3 Double-click your partner's contact	To open it.
Observe the People Pane	The People Pane should contain at least a status message saying that your partner has added you as a colleague.
Observe the Web page address	The address corresponds to your partner's My Site page on the SharePoint server.
4 Click the Web page address	To visit your partner's page. You should see the picture he or she chose, along with the status update and profile information he or she entered.
5 Close the tab	In Internet Explorer.
Minimize Internet Explorer	
6 Close the contact window	
7 In the Navigation pane, click **Contacts**	

The My Site folder is also available in the Contacts folder view.

Topic B: Staying informed with RSS

Explanation

Really Simple Syndication (RSS) feeds give you an easy way to monitor sources of news, blogs (Web logs), and other frequently updated content. RSS content is distributed by publishers in a standard XML file format.

The delivery mechanism for RSS content is known as an *RSS feed*. Other names for RSS feeds are "Web feeds," "XML feeds," "RSS channels," and "syndicated content."

To read RSS feeds, you need to have one of the client software programs, which are known as *RSS aggregators* or RSS readers. Outlook includes the functionality of an RSS aggregator.

Typically with RSS, your reader automatically retrieves summaries of content. Then you decide which articles you want to read and you click an article link. At that time, the full content of the article is retrieved. The article might be displayed within your RSS reader or within your Web browser.

Thanks to the standard XML file format, you can use a single tool to view multiple RSS feeds. It makes no difference that such feeds come from multiple sources. As long as they use one of the various standard RSS XML standards, your reader will be able to retrieve the content and display it for you.

Subscribing to RSS feeds

To subscribe to an RSS feed, you must first find its address. You can find new RSS feeds in several ways. On some Web sites, you might see an orange RSS/XML button or an RSS icon. When you click these buttons in some Web browsers, such as Microsoft Internet Explorer, you can subscribe to the associated feed. You can also find RSS feeds by using a feed search site. These Web sites—such as Syndic8.com and Search4RSS.com—maintain large listings of available RSS feeds.

If you already know the Web address (URL) of an RSS feed, you can enter it within Outlook to subscribe to the feed. Here's how:

1   Display the Folder list.
2   Right-click the RSS Feeds folder and choose Add a New RSS Feed.
3   Enter the URL for the RSS feed and click Add.
4   Click Yes and then click Close.

You can subscribe to a feed without typing or copying and pasting the URL into Outlook. Follow these steps:

1   Use Internet Explorer to visit the Web site that publishes the feed.
2   Click the RSS feed link that the site provides. Some sites display a pop-up window or new page listing all of the feeds they publish. If so, select a feed and click its subscribe button.
3   Internet Explorer displays the contents of the feed. In that window, click "Subscribe to this feed." Then click Subscribe.
4   In Outlook, click the File tab and then click Open.
5   Click Import.
6   Select "Import RSS Feeds from the Common Feed List" and click Next.
7   Check the feed you subscribed to in Internet Explorer and click Next.
8   Click Finish. The feed is added to your RSS Feeds folder.

Do it!

B-1: Subscribing to RSS feeds

Here's how	Here's why
To perform this activity, students must be connected to the Internet. 1 In the Navigation pane, right click **RSS Feeds** and choose **Add a New RSS Feed...**	(If the RSS Feeds folder is not visible, click the Folder List button at the bottom of the Navigation pane to display it.) To open the New RSS Feed dialog box.
2 Enter **http://my.abcnews.go.com/rsspublic/fp_rss20.xml**	
Click **Add**	To add an RSS feed to ABC News Top Stories.
Click **Yes**	To confirm that you want to add the feed. Recent headlines are displayed in the Folder Contents list. The title, date and time, and a summary of the selected news item are displayed in the Reading pane.
3 Observe the Folder list	 The title of the feed you added is displayed, along with the number of unread articles.
4 Switch to or open Internet Explorer	
5 Visit **http://www.skyandtelescope.com/**	
At the time of this writing, the link was in the left column, about halfway down the page. Click where indicated	To open a list of RSS feeds published by *Sky and Telescope* magazine.
6 Next to News stories, click **XML**	The link opens in a new browser window.
7 Click **Subscribe to this feed**	
8 Click **Subscribe**	
9 Close the Internet Explorer windows containing the feed's contents and the window listing the feeds published at this site	
Minimize Internet Explorer	

10 Switch to Outlook	Recent articles from ABC News appear.
11 Click the **File** tab and click **Open**	
12 Click **Import**	
13 Select **Import RSS Feeds from the Common Feed List** and click **Next**	
Check **SkyandTelescope.com's Most Recent News Stories**	
Click **Next**	
Click **Finish**	The RSS feed is added to your RSS Feeds folder.

Articles and updates

Explanation

You can update the content of an RSS feed that you're subscribed to by clicking the Send/Receive All Folders button on the Quick Access toolbar. To read articles in a feed, simply click their titles in the Folder Contents list. Most RSS feeds include a title, perhaps a brief summary of the full article, and a link to the full article. Clicking that link opens your browser and takes you to the feed publisher's Web site.

You can also download a full article to Outlook and then view it in Outlook. With this method, you don't have to open a separate program, but it adds a few extra steps to the process of reading an article.

Do it!

B-2:   Reading a story and updating a feed

Here's how	Here's why
1 In Outlook, select **SkyandTelescope.com's Most Recent News Stories**	In the RSS Feeds folder. The stories in the feed are displayed in the Folder Contents List.
2 Select any story	Click it in the Folder Contents List.
3 Click **View article...**	Internet Explorer opens and the article is loaded into a new tab.
4 Switch back to Outlook	
5 Right-click the headline and choose **Download Content, Download article**	Posted On: Tue 6/8/2010 4:40 AM Feed: SkyandTelescope.com's Most 📧 Message 📄 Full article.htm (76 KB) The article is downloaded and presented as if it were an attachment to an e-mail message.
6 Double-click **Full article.htm**	You are prompted that you should open attachments from only trusted sources.
Click **Open**	Internet Explorer opens with the contents of the article displayed.
7 Observe the Address bar	You're viewing the copy that was downloaded to your computer. You can tell because the address starts with "C:\" rather than with "http://".
8 Close Internet Explorer	Close all tabs.

Changing and removing RSS feeds

Explanation   You can change the name of a feed, the delivery location, and the way the feed processes downloads. To change a feed's options:

1 Click the File tab, click Account Settings, and choose Account Settings to open the Account Settings dialog box.

2 Click the RSS Feeds tab.

3 Select the subscription you want to modify and click Change.

4 Make your changes in the RSS Feed Options dialog box, shown in Exhibit 1-3, and click OK.

Exhibit 1-3: The RSS Feed Options dialog box

Emptying and cleaning up an RSS feed

You can delete individual articles from an RSS feed. Simply select an article and press the Delete key. You can Shift+click articles to select a set of them, and then press Delete. Outlook does not provide a one-button means to delete all of the articles you have read. However, you can perform a custom search for all read items in the folder, select them all, and delete them.

Outlook does provide a simple way to delete all messages in a feed (including both read and unread articles). Right-click the feed and choose Delete All.

Removing RSS feeds

You can remove RSS feeds when you want to end your subscription. Outlook provides two methods for unsubscribing from a feed:

- Open the Account Settings dialog box and click the RSS Feeds tab. Then select the feed and click Remove. The feed is removed, but downloaded RSS items are not removed from the RSS Feeds folder.

- In the RSS Feeds folder in the Folder list, right-click the feed and choose Delete Folder. Then click Yes. The folder, its contents, and your subscription to the feed are removed.

Do it!

B-3: Changing and removing RSS feeds

Here's how	Here's why
1 Click the **File** tab	To display the Account Information page.
Click **Account Settings** and choose **Account Settings...**	To open the Account Settings dialog box.
2 Click the **RSS Feeds** tab	
3 Select **ABC News Top Stories**	You'll change the settings for this feed.
4 Click **Change**	To open the RSS Feed Options dialog box, shown in Exhibit 1-3.
Under Downloads, check **Download the full article as an .html attachment**	To download the full articles as attachments to the RSS item.
Click **OK**	
5 Select **SkyandTelescope.com's Most Recent News Stories**	
Click **Remove**	To remove this feed.
Click **Yes**	To confirm that you want to remove the feed.
6 Click **Close**	
7 In Mail, expand RSS Feeds	If necessary.
8 Right-click **ABC News Top Stories**	
Choose **Delete Folder**	
Click **Yes**	The folder, its contents, and your subscription are deleted. The default explanatory page is displayed after a momentary pause.

Unit summary: Collaboration

Topic A

In this topic, you learned that you can use the **Outlook Social Connector** to display your colleagues' social networking updates in the **People Pane**. You learned how to connect to your social networking account. Then you learned how to connect to colleagues and view their **status updates**. You used **SharePoint**, but learned that the OSC supports connections to LinkedIn, MySpace, and other social networks.

Topic B

In this topic, you learned that you can use Outlook to subscribe to **RSS feeds** and read the articles they contain. You learned that Outlook is an **RSS reader**, also called an aggregator. You subscribed to RSS feeds. Then you learned that you can open and read RSS items just as you would with e-mail messages. Finally, you learned how to unsubscribe from RSS feeds.

Independent practice activity

In this activity, you will work with a partner to explore how SharePoint profile updates are reflected in the People Pane, thanks to the OSC. You will also practice subscribing to, reading, and unsubscribing from an RSS feed.

The files for this activity are in Student Data folder **Unit 1\Unit summary**.

1 Log onto your My Site.

2 Update your profile picture. (*Hint:* In the top-right corner, click your user name and choose My Profile.)

3 Wait until your partner has done the same.

4 Compose a message to your partner. His or her new profile picture might be visible if the server has updated the profile information. If it isn't, close the message, wait a few minutes, and try again.

5 Add an RSS feed to **http://dsc.discovery.com/news/topstories.xml**.

6 Verify that the Discovery feed downloaded RSS items to your RSS Feeds folder.

7 Forward an RSS feed item from Discovery as an e-mail to your partner.

8 Delete an RSS article.

9 Delete the RSS feed folder for SkyandTelescope.com.

Review questions

1 True or false? The OSC enables you to post status updates to your social networking account from within Outlook.

False. You can monitor updates within Outlook. But you need to use your social networking system's tools to post updates.

2 Name a social network that you can link to with the OSC.

At the time of this writing, connectors were available for SharePoint, LinkedIn, and MySpace.

3 OSC updates are displayed in the _____ _____.

People Pane

4 Connecting to a colleague via the OSC is a two-stage process. What is the first stage?

You must connect to your social networking account by configuring the OSC with your account details (URL, user name, and password).

5 Connecting to a colleague via the OSC is a two-stage process. What is the second stage?

You must connect to your colleague. Depending on the social network, he or she might need to approve the connection.

6 True or false? The OSC displays updates instantly, as soon as they are posted.

False. The frequency of updates depends on the connector and the settings configured on the social networking system.

7 Before you can subscribe to an RSS feed, what kind of software do you need?

You need to have an RSS reader, also called an aggregator. Outlook can function as an RSS aggregator.

8 What file format is used for RSS content?

A HTML

B PDF

C DOC

D XML

9 Name one RSS feed search site.

Answers might include:

* *Syndic8.com*

* *CompleteRSS.com*

* *Search4RSS.com*

10 What are some other names for RSS feeds?

Answer will vary, but might include:

* *Web feeds*

* *XML feeds*

* *RSS channels*

* *Syndicated content*

11 How can you add an RSS feed in Outlook?

You can right-click the RSS Feeds folder and choose Add a New RSS Feed, or visit the desired Web site, click its RSS feed link, and click "Subscribe to this feed." You can also use the RSS Feeds tab in the Account Settings dialog box.

Unit 2

Mailbox management

Unit time: 60 minutes

Complete this unit, and you'll know how to:

A Manage the contents of your mailbox to stay within the quota set by your administrator.

B Archive messages, both manually and automatically, to local files or to your archive mailbox.

Topic A: Managing your mailbox

This topic covers the following Microsoft Office Specialist exam objectives for Outlook 2010.

#	Objective
1.2	**Manipulate item tags**
	1.2.5 View message properties
2.1	**Create and send e-mail messages**
	2.1.6 Specify the Sent Items folder
3.1	**Clean up the mailbox**
	3.1.1 View mailbox size
	3.1.2 Save message attachments
	3.1.4 Ignore a conversation
	3.1.5 Use cleanup tools

Mailbox quotas

Explanation

Everything has a limit, and that includes your Outlook Inbox. Your mail administrator has probably set a *quota*—a limit on the amount of space your Inbox and related folders can consume. There are actually three limits your administrator can set:

- **Issue warning** — When you reach this limit, Exchange will send you an e-mail warning that you have neared the quota on your account.
- **Prohibit send** — When you reach this larger mailbox size, Exchange will prevent you from sending messages.
- **Prohibit send and receive** — At the third, and typically highest, size limit, Exchange will prevent you from sending or receiving messages.

To avoid hitting these limits, you should regularly clean out old and unnecessary messages from your mailbox.

Do it!

A-1:   Importing messages so you have data to manage

The files for this activity are in Student Data folder **Unit 2\Topic A**.

Here's how	Here's why
1 Click the **File** tab and click **Open**	You will import a set of messages so that you can manage and delete them during this topic's activities.
2 Click **Import**	
3 Select **Import from another program or file**	If necessary.
Click **Next**	
4 Select **Outlook Data File (.pst)**	
Click **Next**	
5 Click **Browse**	
6 Navigate to the current topic folder	
Select **Mail data**	
Click **Open**	
7 Select **Allow duplicates to be created**	
Click **Next**	
8 Click **Finish**	The messages in this file have been imported into your Inbox.

Cleanup strategies

Explanation

Objective 3.1

There are various strategies for managing the size of your mailbox. Some of them include:

- Deleting messages or attachments you no longer need
- Deleting the contents of automatic folders, including the Deleted Items, Sent Items, and Junk E-Mail folders
- Cleaning up messages and conversations
- Archiving messages to preserve them, while removing them from your mailbox
- Compacting your mailbox file to eliminate wasted space

Deleting messages or attachments

Of the techniques, the simplest is to delete messages you no longer need. Your company might have retention requirements that prohibit you from deleting messages whenever you want. If not, you are free to delete unnecessary messages to free space in your inbox.

You can delete an attachment while keeping the message. You might do so after saving or printing the attached file. Right-click the item and choose Remove Attachment.

Mailbox Cleanup

Objective 3.1.5

You can use the Mailbox Cleanup tool to find older items and then delete, move, or archive them. First, click the File tab to display the Account Information page. Then, click the Cleanup Tools button and choose Mailbox Cleanup to open the Mailbox Cleanup dialog box, shown in Exhibit 2-1.

With this dialog box, you can search for old or large mailbox items, which you can then delete. The dialog box also offers quick access to other cleanup operations, such as determining your mailbox's size, emptying the Deleted Items folder, and so forth.

Exhibit 2-1: The Mailbox Cleanup dialog box

Determining usage

Objective 3.1.1

Outlook provides a couple of ways to determine the amount of space your mailbox is consuming. The easiest way is to click the File tab. In the Mailbox Cleanup section of the Account Information page, Outlook displays both the current usage and your quota limit. But this is just one overall figure for your usage.

To determine more precisely what is consuming the space, you need a different technique:

1 Click the File tab.

2 Click Cleanup Tools and choose Mailbox Cleanup to open the Mailbox Cleanup dialog box.

3 Click View Mailbox Size to open the Folder Size dialog box. It lists each of your folders and their sizes. The Size column lists the size of just the specific folder. The Total Size lists the size of the folder and the subfolders it contains.

Message properties

Objective 1.2.5

When cleaning your mailbox, you might want to see detailed information about a particular e-mail message. Such information might help you decide whether to keep, archive, or delete the message. To view message properties:

1 Open the message (you can't simply preview it in the Reading pane).

2 In the Message window, click the File tab.

3 In the Info pane, scroll down to the Properties section. The message's size is displayed here.

4 Click Properties to open the message's Properties dialog box. It displays the message's headers, as well as various settings that were applied to the message when it was sent.

5 Click Close when you're done.

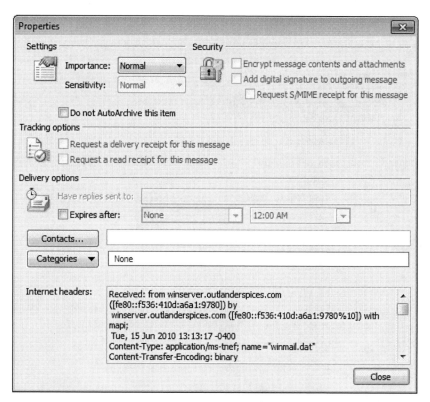

Exhibit 2-2: A message's Properties dialog box

Do it!

A-2:   Deleting messages and attachments

Here's how	Here's why
1 Double-click the **Second photo** message	To open the message.
2 Click the **File** tab	You will view the message's properties to determine whether you should keep, archive, or delete the message.
Objective 1.2.5 Scroll down to the Properties section	**Properties** Set and view advanced options ■ Size: 1 MB The message's size is displayed.
Objective 1.2.5 3 Click **Properties**	To open the message's Properties dialog box. It displays the message headers, along with Importance, Sensitivity, and other details.
Click **Close**	To close the Properties dialog box.
4 Close the Message window	To return to your Inbox.

Objective 3.1.1

5   Click the **File** tab

Mailbox Cleanup
Manage the size of your r
archiving.

■   1.99 GB free of 2 GB

To display the Account Information page. The size of your mailbox is shown in the Mailbox Cleanup section.

TIPS✓   *Or you can right-click your account name, choose Data File Properties, and click the Folder Size button.*

Objectives 3.1.1, 3.1.5

6   Click **Cleanup Tools**

Choose **Mailbox Cleanup...**   To open the Mailbox Cleanup dialog box.

Click **View Mailbox Size**   To open the Folder Size dialog box.

7   Compare the Size and Total Size values for each folder   If you have no subfolders, the two values should match for each of the items. Folders with subfolders will have a larger Total Size than Size.

8   Click **Close** twice   To close the dialog boxes.

Click the **Home** tab

9   In your Inbox, scroll down and select the oldest message, with the subject **Welcome to Outlook 2010**   This represents an old message, the kind you'd periodically look for and delete from your Inbox.

10   Press (*DELETE*)   The message is deleted.

11   Open the message with the subject **Spice photos**   This message contains an attachment.

Objective 3.1.2

12   Right-click the attachment and choose **Save As**

Save the file in your Documents folder   Now that you've saved a copy in your Documents folder, you no longer need the copy in the e-mail message. You'll delete it.

13   Right-click the attachment and choose **Remove Attachment**   The attachment is deleted. The rest of the message is preserved.

14   Close the message window

Click **Yes**   To save your changes to the message. It is still in your Inbox, but no longer has an attachment.

Deleting the contents of automatic folders

Explanation

Outlook maintains various folders that it populates somewhat automatically. For example, by default, a copy of every message you send is saved in the Sent Items folder. Items you delete are moved to the Deleted Items folder, rather than being instantly erased. And junk messages are stored in the Junk E-Mail folder just in case they're not actually junk.

These folders consume space in your mailbox. You should regularly empty these folders, or at least delete items you no longer need. You can also adjust the automatic save options so that you retain less clutter in the first place.

Sent Items

You can turn off the option to save copies of messages you send, but otherwise, you have little control over the action.

1   Click the File tab and click Options to open the Outlook Options dialog box.
2   In the left pane, click Mail; then scroll down to the Save Messages section in the right pane.

Objective 2.1.6

3   Check or clear "Save copies of messages in the Sent Items folder" to configure the action as you desire.
4   Click OK.

Deleted Items

You can configure Outlook to delete the contents of your Deleted Items folder automatically each time you exit the program.

1   Open the Outlook Options dialog box.
2   Click Advanced.
3   In the Outlook start and exit section, check or clear the "Empty Deleted Items folders when exiting Outlook" option.
4   Click OK.

A trick is to not send a message to the Deleted Items folder in the first place. Select the item you want to delete. Then, while holding the Shift key, press the Delete key. You'll be asked whether you want to permanently delete the item. If you click Yes, the item is deleted rather than being moved to the Deleted Items folder.

Junk E-Mail

You should regularly inspect the contents of your Junk E-Mail folder. If any items there are not junk, move them to another folder. Then delete the remaining items.

If you trust Outlook's filtering tools to always correctly distinguish junk from legitimate messages, you can configure the filter to delete messages automatically. On the Home tab of the Inbox, click Junk and choose Junk E-Mail Options. Then check the "Permanently delete suspected junk e-mail" box.

Do it!

A-3: Deleting the contents of automatic folders

Here's how	Here's why
1 Right-click **Sent Items** and choose **Delete All**	You'll start your cleanup by deleting all of the items from the Sent Items folder.
Click **Yes**	The messages are moved to your Deleted Items folder.
2 Open the Outlook Options dialog box	
In the left pane, click **Mail**	
Scroll to the "Save messages" section	This section contains options for managing how copies of messages are saved.
3 Clear **Save copies of messages in the Sent Items folder**	With this option unchecked, Outlook won't save copies of the e-mail messages that you send.
Click **OK**	To save your changes.
4 Right-click **Deleted Items** and choose **Empty Folder**	
Click **Yes**	The folder's contents are deleted.
5 Select your Inbox	If necessary.
6 Select the **Spice Photos** message	This is the message you deleted the attachment from.
7 Press (SHIFT) + (DELETE)	
Click **Yes**	To confirm that you want to delete this message instantly, rather than sending it to the Deleted Items folder.
8 Select **Deleted Items**	The folder is empty.
9 Select **Junk E-Mail**	The folder is most likely empty. You should regularly review the contents of this folder. Move legitimate messages to other folders, and delete the rest.
10 On the Ribbon, click **Junk**	In the Delete group.
Choose **Junk E-Mail Options...**	To open the Junk E-Mail Options dialog box.

11 Observe the "Permanently delete" option	It's not recommended, but you could configure Outlook to delete suspected junk e-mail rather than putting it in the Junk E-Mail folder.
Click **Cancel**	

Cleaning up messages and conversations

Explanation

Objectives 3.1.4, 3.1.5

Imagine this scenario: You send a message to a co-worker. She responds to you, which means that her message to you includes a copy of your original note. You respond to her, and she replies back. Her final note includes two copies of your original note, her original reply, plus her new text. You also have a copy of each of the messages you sent in your Sent Items folder.

Outlook 2010 includes a new automated Clean Up feature that can help you prevent this sort of redundancy and wasted space. When you clean up a folder or conversation, Outlook scans all of the messages and attempts to identify and delete duplicated content. The aim of the Clean Up function is to retain a single copy of each message.

To clean up, on the Home tab, click Clean Up. Then choose one of these three options:

- **Clean Up Conversation** — Cleans up all of the messages in a "thread" (conversation).
- **Clean Up Folder** — Cleans up all messages in the folder, but not in any subfolders.
- **Clean Up Folder & Subfolders** — Cleans up all messages in the folder and its subfolders.

Do it!

Objectives 3.1.4, 3.1.5

A-4: Cleaning up duplicate messages

Here's how	Here's why
1 Select your Inbox	
2 Select the **Lunch party on Friday** message	This is a short message describing the planning for an upcoming party.
3 Select each of the replies to this message	(The replies include RE: in the subject and are listed above the original.) Each of the replies includes the original text. You have multiple copies of the same text wasting space in your Inbox.
4 Click where indicated	Arrange By: Date
Choose **Show as Conversations**	
Click **This folder**	To arrange just this folder by conversations. Arranging by conversations is not required for using the Clean Up function, but it shows how these messages are related and illustrates how duplicates arise during an e-mail exchange.
5 On the Ribbon, in the Delete group, click **Clean Up**	
Choose **Clean Up Folder**	
Click **Clean Up Folder**	Duplicate items are moved to the Deleted Items folder.
6 Select the **Deleted Items** folder	All but the last message in the "Lunch party on Friday" thread are deleted. Any other duplicate messages are also deleted and moved here.
7 Select **Inbox**	
8 Arrange the folder by date, but not in conversations	Click the header and choose Show as Conversations.

Compacting mailboxes

Explanation

Objective 3.1.5

As you send, receive, delete, and move messages over time, your mailbox can come to use storage space inefficiently. When this happens, your mailbox uses more space than is actually required to store the messages it contains. You can compact your mailbox to reclaim this wasted space.

To compact your mailbox:

1　Open the Account Settings dialog box.

2　Click the Data Files tab, select your account, and click Settings.

3　On the Advanced tab, click Outlook Data File Settings.

4　Click Compact Now.

5　Click OK twice and then click Close to close all of the dialog boxes.

Do it!

Objective 3.1.5

A-5:　Compacting your mailbox

Here's how	Here's why
1　Click the **File** tab	
Click **Account Settings** and choose **Account Settings...**	To open the Account Settings dialog box.
2　Click the **Data Files** tab	
Click **Settings**	To open the Microsoft Exchange dialog box.
3　Click the **Advanced** tab	
Click **Outlook Data File Settings**	To open the Outlook Data File Settings dialog box.
4　Click **Compact Now**	To compact your mailbox files and reclaim wasted space.
5　Click **OK** twice	
Click **Close**	To close the dialog boxes.

Topic B: Archiving your mail

This topic covers the following Microsoft Office Specialist exam objectives for Outlook 2010.

#	Objective
3.1	**Clean up the mailbox**
	3.1.3 Save message in an external format
	3.1.5 Use cleanup tools

Overview of archiving

Explanation

Archiving is the process of periodically saving old messages in a file on your computer or in a special *archive mailbox* on the Exchange server. Archiving reclaims space in your mailbox while preserving old messages in case you need them.

Objective 3.1.5

In earlier versions of Outlook, your only option was to archive to a file on your computer. Although this method freed space in your mailbox, if that file were deleted or became corrupted, you would lose your archived messages.

Outlook 2010 introduces the archive mailbox. This is a special, secondary mailbox that can be enabled for your account. If your administrator has enabled the archive mailbox, you can archive messages in it rather than in a file. Your archive mailbox will be stored on the Exchange server and will be backed up when the server is backed up.

Archiving options

Outlook offers the option to archive to a file or to the archive mailbox. When archiving to a local file, you can do so manually or configure Outlook to archive your data automatically. Your administrator can configure a retention policy that will automatically archive your messages to the archive mailbox.

Manual archiving to a file

With the manual archiving method, you specify which messages to archive and then direct Outlook to perform the archiving operation.

Objective 3.1.3

1 Click the File tab. On the Account Information page, click Cleanup Tools and choose Archive to open the Archive dialog box, shown in Exhibit 2-3.
2 Under "Archive this folder and all subfolders," select the folder you want to archive.
3 From the "Archive items older than" list, select a date.
4 In the Archive file box, enter a name for the archive file. Alternatively, use the Browse button to specify a name and location for the archive file.
5 Click OK.

Exhibit 2-3: The Archive dialog box

B-1: Archiving mail messages to a local file

The files for this activity are in Student Data folder **Unit 2\Topic B**.

Here's how	Here's why
1 Click the **File** tab	To display the Account Information page.
Click **Cleanup Tools** and choose **Archive...**	To open the Archive dialog box. The Inbox is selected by default.
2 Click as shown	Archive items older than: Wed 3/17/2010
	☐ Include items with "Do not AutoArchive" checked
	By default, the date shown is three months before today's date.
In the Date Navigator, click **Today**	To jump to today's date.
Display the Date Navigator again and select tomorrow's date	You'll archive items older than tomorrow, which means that you'll archive any messages you received today. If you selected today's date, you would archive messages received yesterday and earlier.
3 Click **Browse**	To open the Open Personal Folders dialog box. In the File name box, "archive" appears. This is the default archive file name.
Navigate to the current topic folder	Student Data folder Unit 2\Topic B.
4 Click **OK** twice	All items in the Inbox are saved in the file archive.pst.
Click **Yes**	To confirm that you want to archive all of the items in the folder.
5 Click the **Home** tab	It might take a moment, but all of the messages in your inbox are removed and stored in a new Archives folder.
6 In the Folder List pane, expand **Archives**	This folder contains the archived versions of your Inbox, Deleted Items, and Search folders.
7 In the Folder List pane, right-click **Archives**	
Choose **Close "Archives"**	This step doesn't delete the Archives file from your computer. It just removes it from the Folder list.

Restoring archived messages

Explanation

Objective 3.1

In general, you can work with archived messages just as you would work with those in your Inbox. You can reply to or forward archived messages, and so forth. If you have closed your archive folder, however, you won't be able to access those messages.

To restore archived messages stored in a file, you'll need to import the file into Outlook. To do so:

1   Click the File tab and then click Open.

2   Click Open Outlook Data file.

3   Navigate to and select the archive file, and click OK.

The archive file will be opened, and its contents will be displayed in a folder named after the file. For example, if the file is named "archive," the folder will also be called "archive." You can rename it in Outlook.

Do it!

B-2: Opening an archive file

The files for this activity are in Student Data folder **Unit 2\Topic B**.

Objective 3.1

Here's how	Here's why
1 Click the **File** tab and click **Open**	
2 Click **Open Outlook Data File**	
Navigate to the current topic folder	Student Data folder Unit 2\Topic B.
3 Click **archive** and then click **OK**	
4 Expand **archive**	In the Folder list.
Within the archive folder, select **Inbox**	Your archived messages are again available, though the folder now has your file's name rather than the name "Archives."
5 Select all of the messages in the archived Inbox folder	
Drag them to your Inbox	To restore them to your Inbox.
6 Close (remove) the archive folder	(Right-click the folder and choose Close "archive.") To remove it from the Folder list.

Tell students they're doing this so they have messages in their Inbox for upcoming activities.

Automatic archiving to a file

Explanation

Objectives 3.1.3, 3.1.5

You can schedule the archiving of your messages with the AutoArchive feature. For example, you can set AutoArchive to happen every 90 days. When setting the AutoArchive option, you can also set options to delete old archived items and to be notified before archiving begins.

You can define AutoArchive settings for your entire mailbox or individually for specific folders. For example, you might archive Calendar items every month and delete the old items, while archiving your Inbox quarterly and saving old messages.

To configure AutoArchive settings for your entire mailbox:

1   Click the File tab and then click Options to open the Outlook Options dialog box.
2   Click Advanced.
3   Click AutoArchive Settings to open the AutoArchive dialog box, shown on the left in Exhibit 2-4.

To configure AutoArchive settings for a specific folder:

1   Right-click the folder and choose Properties.
2   Click the AutoArchive tab, which is shown on the right in Exhibit 2-4.

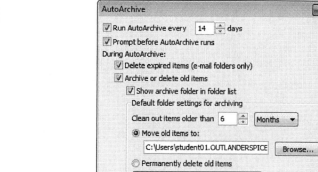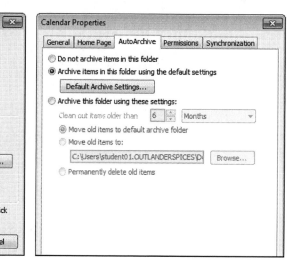

Exhibit 2-4: The AutoArchive dialog box and the AutoArchive tab in the Calendar Properties dialog box

Do it!

Objectives 3.1.3, 3.1.5

B-3: Archiving mail messages to a file automatically

Here's how	Here's why
1 Open the Outlook Options dialog box	
Click **Advanced**	
2 Click **AutoArchive Settings**	To open the AutoArchive dialog box. By default, the settings shown in Exhibit 2-4 are applied.
3 Check **Run AutoArchive every**	To enable AutoArchive. The default frequency is every 14 days.
Edit the box next to "Run AutoArchive every" to read **60**	
4 Edit the box next to "Clean out items older than" to read **60**	
From the list next to "Clean out items older than," select **Days**	(If necessary.) To AutoArchive items older than 60 days.
5 Click **Browse**	To open the Find Personal Folders dialog box. In the File name box, "archive" appears. By default, archived items are saved in a file with this name.
Navigate to the current topic folder	Student Data folder Unit 2\Topic B.
Edit the File name box to read **auto archive**	You'll save the file as auto archive.pst so that the previous PST file isn't overwritten.
Click **OK**	To save the file and close the Find Personal Folders dialog box.
6 Click **OK**	To close the AutoArchive dialog box.
7 Click **OK**	To close the Outlook Options dialog box. Automatic archiving is now scheduled to happen every 60 days.
8 Click the **Home** tab	If necessary.
Select your Inbox	If necessary.

TIPS *Tell students that they can also use the spin control to change the value in the box.*

Help students navigate to the current topic folder.

The archive mailbox

Explanation

Objective 3.1.5

As mentioned previously, Outlook 2010 introduces the archive mailbox. With this secondary mailbox enabled for your account, you can archive messages in a storage location on the Exchange server, and your archive mailbox will be backed up when the server is backed up.

Another benefit of the archive mailbox being on the mail server is that you can access it via *Outlook Web Access* (OWA). You can also access it when you log onto Outlook from another computer. Your archives are thus available from any computer, not just the one where you stored the archive PST file.

You can manually archive to the archive mailbox by simply copying or moving messages to it. The administrator must configure retention policies to automatically archive messages to your archive mailbox.

To use the archive mailbox feature, your organization must purchase *client access licenses* (CALs) for each user. There are various configuration steps that your mail administrator must perform to set up archive mailboxes and retention policies. Check with your administrator to see if your organization has purchased CALs so that you can take advantage of the archive mailbox.

Do it!

Objective 3.1.5

B-4:   Archiving to the archive mailbox

Here's how	Here's why
1 Expand **Archive – student##@outlanderspices.com**	
	To expand your archive mailbox.
2 Right-click your archive mailbox	
Choose **New Folder…**	To open the Create New Folder dialog box.
3 Type **My archive** and click **OK**	To create a folder in your archive mailbox.
4 Select your Inbox	If necessary.
5 Drag a message from your Inbox to **My archive**	To manually archive a message to your archive mailbox. If you were to log on via OWA, you could access this message.
6 Collapse your archive mailbox	Click the triangle to hide the folder's contents.

Unit summary: Mailbox management

Topic A   In this topic, you learned how to manage the contents of your mailbox. You learned various strategies for staying within your mailbox **quota**. For example, you learned how to delete messages and attachments, **empty automatic folders**, **clean up** conversations, and **compact** your mailbox.

Topic B   In this topic, you learned how to **archive** mail, both manually and automatically. You archived messages to a local file and to the archive mailbox. You also configured **AutoArchive** settings to enable periodic archiving of your mailbox.

Independent practice activity

In this activity, you will configure automatic archiving and work with attachments.

1 Configure AutoArchive to automatically archive your entire mailbox every 30 days. Make sure old items are moved to the archive file rather than deleted. Archive to a file named **AutoArchive.pst** in your Documents folder.

2 Configure automatic archiving on your Calendar folder to run every 30 days. Make sure old items are deleted rather than saved.

3 Find a message in your Inbox or archive that has an attachment. Save the attachment in your Documents folder. Then delete the attachment from the e-mail message.

4 Configure Outlook to save copies of messages that you send in the Sent Items folder.

Review questions

1 Deleting unneeded messages and attachments is simple and frees space in your mailbox. Why do you think it's not typically the most effective technique?

Users fail to do it. They forget or get too busy and fail to delete old messages.

2 Periodically, you should check the _____ _____ folder to make sure legitimate e-mail messages weren't stored there. Then you should empty this folder.

Junk E-Mail

3 Name at least two folders you should periodically empty.

Deleted Items, Sent Items, and Junk E-Mail

4 When you're using the Clean Up function, what three options can you choose from to specify which locations to clean up?

• *Clean Up Conversation*

• *Clean Up Folder*

• *Clean Up Folder & Subfolders*

5 Describe how you can determine the amount of overall space consumed by your mailbox.

You can click the File tab and observe the Mailbox Clean up section of the Account Information page.

6 Which of the following is the term for the process of storing old messages in a separate file on your computer?

   A Archiving

   B Clearing

   C Purging

   D Backing up

7 How do you access the mailbox-wide AutoArchive settings?

   Click the File tab and click Options. Then click Advanced and click AutoArchive Settings.

8 How do you access the folder-specific AutoArchive settings?

   Right-click the folder and choose Properties. Then click the AutoArchive tab.

9 True or false? You can reply to or forward a message in your archive just as you would do with a message in your Inbox.

   True

10 To use the archive mailbox, your organization must purchase a _____ _____ _____ for every user who will use the feature.

   client access license

11 Name an advantage of using the archive mailbox instead of a local file.

   Answers include:

   • *The archive mailbox is on the server, and is therefore backed up with the rest of the server's data.*

   • *You can access your archive mailbox via Outlook Web Access (OWA).*

   • *You can access your archive mailbox from other computers running Outlook 2010.*

12 True or false? Removing an archive folder from the Navigation pane deletes it from your hard drive.

   False. The file is not affected. The folder is simply removed from the pane within Outlook.

Unit 3

The Notes and Journal folders

Unit time: 60 minutes

Complete this unit, and you'll know how to:

A Create, forward, and customize notes.

B Create automatic and manual Journal entries, and open and modify Journal entries.

Topic A: Recording information with notes

This topic covers the following Microsoft Office Specialist exam objectives for Outlook 2010.

#	Objective
1.1	**Apply and manipulate Outlook program options**
	1.1.5 Set Notes and Journal options
1.5	**Print an Outlook item**
	1.5.6 Print multiple notes
6.2	**Create and manipulate Notes**
	6.2.1 Create a note
	6.2.2 Change the current view
	6.2.3 Categorize notes

Creating notes

Explanation

Objectives 6.2.1, 6.2.2, 6.2.3

You can use notes in Outlook as reminders for the activities you need to do. You might also use notes for quickly entering useful ideas and information that you can refer to later. It can be convenient to keep notes with relevant information open on your screen when you work in other applications.

To create a note, activate the Notes pane and click the New Note button on the Home tab. A blank note appears, and you can type your information in it. The current date and time appear in the lower portion of the note. You can double-click a note to open and edit it. When you close a note, its contents are saved automatically.

Do it!

Objectives 6.2.1, 6.2.2, 6.2.3

A-1:   Creating and modifying notes

Here's how	Here's why
1 In the lower portion of the Navigation pane, click ▢	(The Notes button.) To activate the Notes pane.
2 Click **New Note**	To create a note. By default, a note is yellow, and the current date and time appear in the lower portion of it.
Type **Conduct a survey for new clients.**	
3 Click ☒	(In the upper-right corner of the note window.) To close the note. The note is automatically saved and appears as an icon in the Folder Contents list.
4 Double-click the note icon	To open the note.
Place the insertion point as shown	
Press (SPACEBAR)	
Type **Contact Juan Martinez for details.**	
5 In the upper-left corner of the note window, click as shown	
	The note menu appears.
6 Choose **Categorize**, **Blue Category**	To change the color of the note to blue. The Rename Category dialog box appears.
In the Name box, enter **Business**, and then click **Yes**	The first time you use a category, you are prompted to rename it.
Close the note	Click the Close button in the upper-right corner of the note window.

TIPS ✔ *Tell students they can also press Ctrl+N.*

Forwarding notes

Explanation

When working on a project, you might want to share with other team members some useful tips or pieces of information that you've saved in a note. You can forward notes as e-mail attachments. To do so, right-click the note and choose Forward to create an e-mail message. The note appears as an attachment. You can then send the message to your team members.

Do it!

A-2: Forwarding notes

Here's how	Here's why
1 In the Folder Contents list, right-click the Juan Martinez note	Copy Quick Print Forward Categorize ▸ Delete To display a shortcut menu.
2 Choose **Forward**	To create a message. The note appears as an attachment in the Attach box. The subject box shows "FW: Conduct a survey for new clients. Contact Juan Martinez for details."
3 Send the message to your partner	
4 In the Navigation pane, click **Mail**	To activate Mail.
5 Open the new message from your partner	The note is included as an attachment.
6 Double-click the attachment	To open the note. It opens and operates just like a note you create on your computer.
Close the note	Click its "X" button.
7 Close the message window	

Customizing notes

Explanation

Objectives 1.1.5, 6.2.3

You can customize notes by changing their properties, such as size, color, and font. If you have notes for several projects, you can customize the appearance of the notes for each project so you can easily identify them. By default, a note is yellow with a medium size. You can view notes by their color and category.

To change properties for notes:

1 Click the File tab and click Options to open the Outlook Options dialog box.
2 In the left pane, click Notes and Journal. Use the pane on the right, shown in Exhibit 3-1, to configure note and journal options.
3 From the Color list, select the desired color.
4 From the Size list, select a size for the note.
5 Click Font to open the Font dialog box. Select a font and click OK.
6 Click OK.

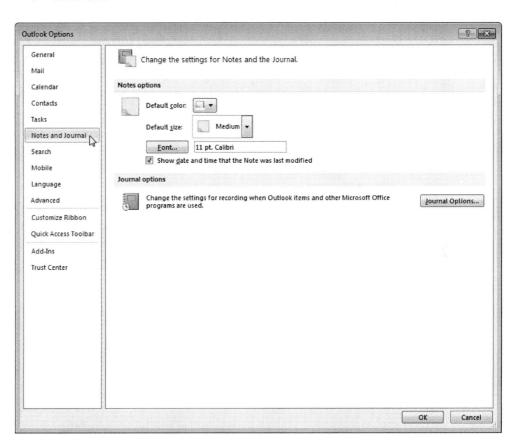

Exhibit 3-1: Setting Notes options in the Outlook Options dialog box

Do it!

Objectives 1.1.5, 6.2.3

A-3: Customizing notes

Here's how	Here's why
1 In the Navigation pane, click ☐	(The Notes button) To activate Notes. You'll change the appearance of your notes.
2 Open the Outlook Options dialog box	
Click **Notes and Journal**	
3 From the Color list, select the pink swatch	To change the color of notes to pink.
From the Size list, select **Small**	To reduce the size of notes.
4 Click **Font**	To open the Font dialog box.
5 In the Font list, select **Candara**	
In the Size list, select **9**	
Click **OK**	To close the Font dialog box and return to the Outlook Options dialog box.
6 Click **OK**	To close the Outlook Options dialog box.
7 On the Ribbon, click **New Note**	
Type **Submit the changed sales policy.**	Submit the changed sales policy. 6/18/2010 10:01
8 Close the note	The new note's icon is pink because this is the default color you specified for new notes. The old note is blue because you assigned it to the Blue category.

Printing notes

Explanation

Objective 1.5.6

Printing notes can be handy when you need to take them with you when you'll be away from your computer. You might also want to print a note if it becomes long and difficult to read on screen. Of course, keep the environment in mind and print only when you need to.

To print a note, select it in Notes view, click the File tab, and click Print. The Print window, shown in Exhibit 3-2, will appear. From here, you can select a printer and other options. Click the Print button to send the print job to your printer.

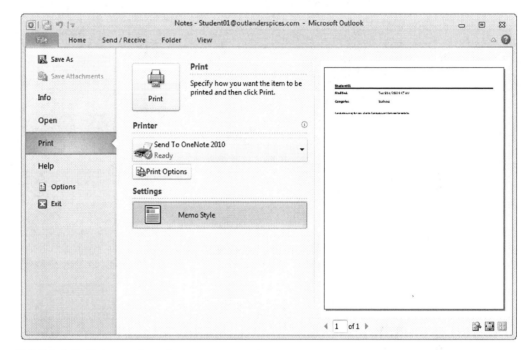

Exhibit 3-2: Print options for a note

To print multiple notes, simply Ctrl+click or Shift+click to select the notes you want to print. Then click the File tab, click Print, and click the Print button. Notes are printed one to a page.

Do it!

A-4:   Printing notes

Here's how	Here's why
1 Click to select the blue note	The first note you created.
2 Click the **File** tab and then click **Print**	To display Print options, shown in Exhibit 3-2.
3 Observe the preview pane	This is a short note and would not fill much space on the page.
4 In the lower-right corner of the window, click where indicated	
	To zoom in the preview area.
Click where indicated	
	To zoom out again.
5 Click the **Home** tab	To return to Notes view.
6 While holding (CTRL), click both notes	To select them both.
7 Click the **File** tab and then click **Print**	Because you have selected multiple notes, the preview is not automatically displayed.
8 Click **Preview**	Notes will be printed one to a page.
9 Click where indicated	
	To preview the printout of the second note.
10 Click the **Home** tab	To return to Notes view.

You don't need a physical printer to complete this activity.

Objective 1.5.6

Assigning contacts to notes

Explanation

You can assign contacts to a note and then send the note as an attachment. If you receive a note with contacts, you need to open the note and then click the note icon. This action opens a menu, from which you choose Contacts to display the names of related contacts. Double-click a name in the box near the Contacts button to open that contact. By using the information in that contact, recipients can update their contact data. You can view the contact information only if the person who sent you the message shares that person's Contacts folder.

To assign a contact to a note:

1   Open a note.
2   Click the note menu icon and choose Contacts to open the Contacts for Note dialog box.
3   Click Contacts to open the Select Contacts dialog box.
4   From the Items list, select a contact. Click OK.
5   Click Close to close the Contacts for Note dialog box.
6   Click the note icon and choose Forward. A message opens with the note as an attachment.
7   Send the message.

A-5:   Assigning a contact to a note

Here's how	Here's why
1 Create a new contact for your partner	(In your inbox, open a message from your partner, and point to your partner's name. Click the View More Options icon and select Add to Outlook Contacts. Click Save & Close.)
Return to the Notes pane	(Click the Notes button.)
2 Double-click the blue note icon	To open the blue note. You'll assign a contact to this note and send it to your partner. Your partner can open it and view the contact information.
3 Click the note menu icon	(Located in the upper-left corner of the note.) To display the menu.
Choose **Contacts...**	To open the Contacts for Note dialog box.
4 Click **Contacts**	To open the Select Contacts dialog box.
In the Items list, select your partner	Items: / Filed As / student02
Click **OK**	
5 Click **Close**	To close the Contacts for Note dialog box.
Click the note menu icon	
Choose **Forward**	To open a message. If a message box appears, asking whether you need to save the item, click OK.
6 Send the message to a student in the class who is not your partner	
7 Close the note	
8 In the Navigation pane, click **Mail**	To activate Mail.
9 Open the new message that you received from another student	
10 Double-click the note icon in the attachment area of the message	To open the note.

If students have performed the social connector activities in an earlier unit, you can also have them copy the contact from their My Site folder into Contacts.

Tell students that they can view a note's full name by selecting the note.

Help students identify someone to send the message to.

11 Click the note menu icon

    Choose **Contacts...**   To open the Contacts for Note dialog box. The
                                              student name that the sender attached is listed in
                                              the contacts box. You could double-click the
                                              name to view the contact details.

    Click **Close**   To close the Contacts for Note dialog box.

12 Close the note

    Close the message

Topic B: Tracking activities with the Journal

This topic covers the following Microsoft Office Specialist exam objectives for Outlook 2010.

#	Objective
1.1	**Apply and manipulate Outlook program options**
	1.1.5 Set Notes and Journal options
6.3	**Create and manipulate Journal entries**
	6.3.1 Automatically record Outlook items
	6.3.2 Automatically record files
	6.3.3 Edit a Journal entry

Creating and using Journal entries

Explanation

Objective 6.3.1

You can use the Journal to manage, document, and track communication related to your contacts. The Journal records the time and date of your communications. For example, you can find out when you received a request for a meeting with a client. The Journal can also record documents in applications such as Word and Excel.

An item created in the Journal folder is called a Journal entry. You can make a Journal entry either manually or automatically. You can modify Journal entries, change Journal views, and assign contacts to Journal entries. Using the Journal, you can track the following Outlook items for your contacts:

- E-mail messages
- Meeting requests
- Meeting responses
- Task requests
- Task responses

Recording Journal entries automatically

Objectives 1.1.5, 6.3.2

You can record files from Office applications such as Word and Excel. To record activities automatically:

1 In the Outlook Options dialog box, click Notes and Journal.
2 Click Journal Options to open the Journal Options dialog box, shown in Exhibit 3-3.
3 Under "Automatically record these items," check the items you want to record automatically.
4 Under "For these contacts," check the desired contacts.
5 Under "Also record files from," check the applications you want to record. These options appear only if you've installed the corresponding Microsoft Office applications.
6 Click OK to apply the settings.
7 Click OK to close the Outlook Options dialog box.

Objective 6.3.2

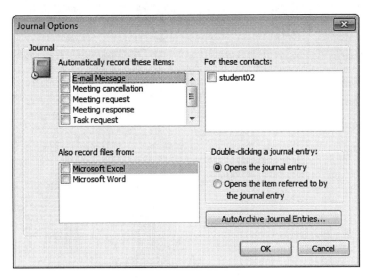

Exhibit 3-3: The Journal Options dialog box

Do it!

B-1: Configuring the Journal to record entries automatically

Objectives 1.1.5, 6.3.1

Here's how	Here's why
1 In the lower-right corner of the Navigation pane, click as shown	To display a menu.

Tell students they'll use the Journal button in an upcoming activity.

Here's how	Here's why
2 Choose **Add or Remove Buttons**, **Journal**	To add the Journal button to the Navigation pane.
Observe the Journal button	It appears at the bottom of the Navigation pane.
3 Open the Outlook Options dialog box	
Click **Notes and Journal**	
Click **Journal Options**	

Tell students they will need to scroll down to check Task response.

Here's how	Here's why
4 Under "Automatically record these items," check all items	Automatically record these items: ☑ Meeting cancellation ☑ Meeting request ☑ Meeting response ☑ Task request ☑ Task response To automatically record details about all of the checked items.
5 Under "For these contacts," check your partner's name	For these contacts: ☑ student02 To automatically record activities related to this contact.

Objective 6.3.2

Here's how	Here's why
6 Observe the "Also record files from" options	Also record files from: ☐ Microsoft Excel ☐ Microsoft Word You can use the Journal to track your work on Office documents.
7 Click **OK**	To close the Journal Options dialog box.
8 Click **OK**	To close the Outlook Options dialog box.

Do it!

Objective 6.3.1

B-2: Creating activity that will be recorded in the Journal

Here's how	Here's why
1 Activate the Calendar	You'll perform an activity to be recorded in the Journal folder.
2 Click **New Meeting**	On the Home tab.
3 In the To box, enter your partner's name	To send the meeting request to your partner.
In the Subject box, enter **Conference on latest sales policy**	
In the Location box, enter **Conference room**	
4 Select a start date and time for next week	Notice that the difference between the start time and the end time is 30 minutes.
Verify that a Reminder is set for 15 minutes	The Reminder list appears in the Options group on the Meeting tab.
Click **Send**	To send the meeting request to your partner.
5 Activate Mail	
6 Double-click the message **Conference on latest sales policy**	To open the message.
7 Click **Accept** and choose **Send the response now**	To accept the meeting request and send the response.

⚠ *Tell students to make sure they don't select the same date and time as their partner.*

Viewing Journal entries

Explanation

Objective 6.3

Activity recorded in the Journal is displayed in the Journal folder. Outlook provides various display options, including the default Timeline view shown in Exhibit 3-4. Change the view by clicking an option in the Current View group on the Home tab of the Journal.

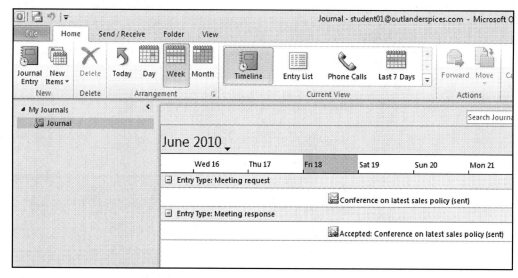

Exhibit 3-4: The Journal's Timeline view

Do it!

Objective 6.3

B-3: Viewing Journal entries

Here's how	Here's why
1 In the Navigation pane, click [icon]	To open the Journal folder. Your entries are displayed in a timeline format, as shown in Exhibit 3-4.
2 In the Current View group on the Home tab, click **Entry List**	To display your Journal entries as a list instead of as a timeline.
Observe the Journal entries	Both the meeting request sent to your partner and your acceptance of your partner's request are recorded in the Journal.
3 In the Current View list, click **Phone calls**	You haven't journaled any phone calls with your partner, so the list is empty.
4 In the Current View list, click **Last 7 Days**	This view also shows Journal entries as a list, but it shows just the entries from the past week.

Using the Journal to record items manually

Explanation

Using the Journal, you can manually track details about activities such as phone calls and faxes, in addition to Outlook items, such as e-mail messages, notes, meeting responses, and meeting cancellations.

To create a Journal entry manually:

Objective 6.3

1 Open the Journal Entry window, shown in Exhibit 3-5, by using one of these techniques:

- In the Journal, on the Home tab, click Journal Entry.
- In most folders, on the Ribbon, click New Items and choose More Items, Journal Entry.
- Press Ctrl+Shift+J.

2 If you're recording activity associated with a phone call or other time-related event, click Start Timer to begin recording the time associated with this entry. When you're done, click Pause Timer.

3 Enter the details associated with this entry. With entries for phone calls, you would typically perform this step after the call has ended.

4 Save and close the Journal entry.

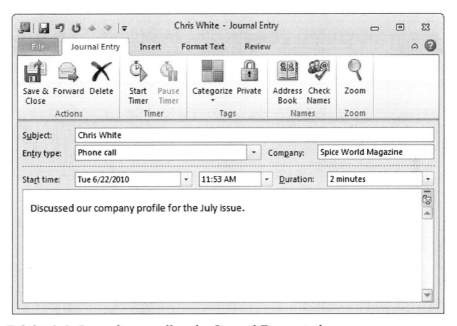

Exhibit 3-5: Recording a call in the Journal Entry window

Students are creating a timer for a mock phone call with a client.

B-4:   Creating a Journal entry manually

Here's how	Here's why
1 Click **Journal Entry**	You create a mock entry for a phone call.
2 Click **Start Timer**	
3 In the Subject box, type **Chris White**	With a real phone call, you'd probably wait until the call was done before entering any details.
4 In the Company box, type **Spice World Magazine**	
5 Click **Pause Timer**	To stop recording time for this entry.
6 In the comments area, type **Discussed our company profile for the July issue.**	
7 Click **Save & Close**	To save the Journal entry and close the Journal Entry window. A new Journal entry appears in the Journal folder.

Reading a Journal entry

Explanation

Journal entries record the time spent on an activity, as well as notes and details you add. Journal entries also retain an association with the event to which they are related. For example, let's say you create a meeting request with a contact with whom you've enabled automatic journaling. Creating that request also creates a Journal entry. You can view the Journal entry to see details about the time spent on that activity. You can also access the meeting entry on your calendar via the Journal entry, thanks to its association with the calendar item.

To view a Journal entry, in order to see the time spent or work details, simply double-click the Journal entry item. You'll open a window like the one shown in Exhibit 3-6.

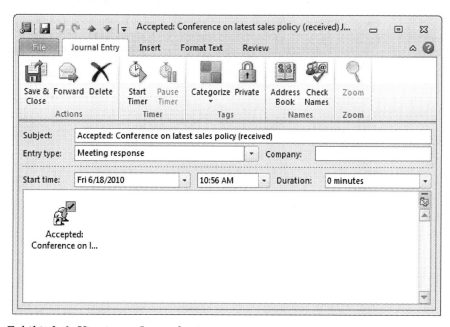

Exhibit 3-6: Viewing a Journal entry

To open the original item recorded by the Journal, right-click the Journal entry and choose Open Item Referred To from the shortcut menu. If you have the Journal entry open, double-click the link it contains. (An example is shown in the comments area in Exhibit 3-6.)

B-5:   Opening a Journal entry and the item it refers to

Here's how	Here's why
1 Double-click **Conference on latest sales policy (sent)**	To open the Journal Entry window, in which you can view details, such as the entry type and duration.
2 Double-click where indicated	You're prompted with a virus warning.
Click **Yes**	To open the Meeting window with which this entry is associated.
3 Close the Meeting window	
Close the Journal entry window	
4 Right-click **Conference on latest sales policy (sent)**	To display a shortcut menu.
5 Choose **Open Item Referred To**	To open the Meeting window with which this entry is associated.
Close the Meeting window	

Editing a Journal entry

Explanation

You can edit a Journal entry in the Journal folder if needed. For example, you might have created a task-related Journal entry. Whenever you work on that task, you can record your time by updating that entry.

To edit a Journal entry:

Objective 6.3.3

1 Open the Journal entry.
2 Modify it as needed. If you're using the Journal to track time, click Start Timer when you open the entry. Then click Pause Timer when you're done working.
3 Click Save & Close.

Do it!

Objective 6.3.3

B-6: Noting work performed with a Journal entry

Here's how	Here's why
1 Create a Journal entry	(Click Journal Entry on the Ribbon.) You'll start by creating an entry that you can then edit.
Enter the details shown	**Subject:** Reviewing the sales policy doc. **Entry type:** Task
Click **Save & Close**	To save your entry. Now you have something to edit.
2 Double-click your new entry	To open it.
3 Click **Start Timer**	You can leave this Journal Entry window open as you do your work. Then, when you take a break or finish the task, you can pause the timer to save the time spent.
4 After a minute or so, click **Pause Timer**	You can enter a time in the Duration field to manually note the time spent on an entry. For example, you'd use that facility for those times that you're not working at your desk.
5 Click **Save & Close**	To save and close the Journal entry.
Observe the Duration column	**Duration** . 2 minutes
	It displays the time you have spent on this activity.

If students don't see a Duration column, have them increase the width of the pane.

Unit summary: The Notes and Journal folders

Topic A

In this topic, you learned that you can create **notes** to save ideas and information for later reference. You learned how to forward and customize notes. Finally, you learned that you can **assign a contact** to a note. When you forward a note that contains a contact, the recipient can view both the note and the contact information.

Topic B

In this topic, you learned that you can track your time with **Journal entries**. You learned how to create Journal entries both automatically and manually. You also learned how to edit a Journal entry, which you'd do to track ongoing work related to an entry.

Independent practice activity

In this activity, you will create and customize a note and create Journal entries automatically and manually.

1 Create a note with the content **Send a fax to William Jones about the new advertising strategy.**

2 Assign the Green category to the note. Rename the Green category as **Marketing**. Close the note.

3 Customize Notes to change the default setting of notes to yellow and to medium size.

4 Create a manual Journal entry. Immediately start the timer. After a minute or so, click Pause Timer. Enter the subject **Call from Leslie Jones** and set the entry type as **Phone call**. Save your changes.

5 Edit your Journal entry. Update the duration to five minutes. Save your changes.

Review questions

1 How do you save a note?

When you close a note, it is saved automatically.

2 How do you view contact information that has been attached to a note and sent to you?

   a Open the message that contains the note.

   b Double-click the note icon to open the note.

   c Click the note menu icon and choose Contacts.

3 How do you change the default color of a note?

   a Open the Outlook Options dialog box.

   b Click Notes and Journal.

   c From the Color list, select the desired color.

   d Click OK.

4 By using the Journal, what kinds of Outlook items can you track for contacts?

Answers include:

- *E-mail messages*
- *Meeting requests*
- *Meeting cancellations*
- *Meeting responses*
- *Task requests*
- *Task responses*

5 True or false? You can use the Start Timer and Pause Timer buttons or the Duration box to record the amount of time you spend in association with a Journal entry.

True

6 How do you open an original item recorded by the Journal?

Right-click the Journal entry and choose Open Item Referred To from the shortcut menu.

7 What is the default view for the Journal folder?

Timeline

8 True or false? The Journal is not enabled by default and you must configure it to enable it.

True

Unit 4

Calendars and contacts

Unit time: 60 minutes

Complete this unit, and you'll know how to:

A Share your calendar with others, delegate authority to access your calendar on your behalf, and synchronize your calendar with SharePoint.

B Share contacts, export lists of contacts, and synchronize your contacts with SharePoint.

Topic A: Managing your calendar

This topic covers the following Microsoft Office Specialist exam objectives for Outlook 2010.

#	Objective
5.3	**Manipulate the Calendar pane**
	5.3.2 Change the calendar color
	5.3.3 Display or hide calendars
	5.3.4 Create a calendar group

Sharing calendars

Explanation

You might need to manage another person's calendar, or you might need to delegate calendar management to someone else. Perhaps you're an administrative assistant and your boss has asked you to book appointments and meetings on her calendar. Maybe you're the boss and you need to permit your assistant to manage your calendar.

Sharing via Exchange

Outlook, when used in conjunction with Exchange Server, offers you three levels of support for shared access to calendars. They are:

- **Sharing** — Enables limited access to your calendar. Use this level to let co-workers and managers see your calendar and keep track of your schedule.

- **Setting calendar permissions** — Enables you to grant read and editing access to your mailbox. This level is useful for enabling someone to manage your calendar.

- **Delegating access** — Is like granting permissions. When you delegate access, you enable others to view and edit your calendar. You also grant permission to send e-mail messages on your behalf (under your name). This level is most appropriate in a scenario in which an administrative assistant would send out meeting invitations under your name.

Publishing online

Outlook offers two additional options for sharing your calendar that don't require Exchange Server. They are:

- **Publishing to Office.com** — If you have a Live.com or Office.com user account, you can publish your calendar to the Office.com site. Then you can send people invitations to view your published calendar.

- **Publishing to a WebDAV server** — *WebDAV (Web Distributed Authoring and Versioning)* is a technology that enables applications, such as Outlook, to transmit data to a Web server. If you or your organization has a WebDAV-capable server, you can publish your calendar to it. Permissions and settings on the Web server control who can see your calendar.

Do it!

A-1: Adding an appointment to your calendar

Here's how	Here's why
1 Display your calendar	You're adding an item to your calendar so you have something to view in the upcoming activities.
2 Double-click any time block within the workday	(Between 8:00 AM and 5:00 PM.) To open an Appointment window.
3 Enter an appointment subject	Such as "Dentist appointment."
4 Enter a location	Such as "123 Main St."
5 On the Ribbon, from the Show As list, select **Out of Office**	
6 Click **Save & Close**	

Calendar sharing

Explanation

To share your calendar:

1 In the Navigation pane, under My Calendars, right-click Calendar and choose Share, Share Calendar. A sharing invitation window, as shown in Exhibit 4-1, is displayed.

2 As you would with an e-mail message, address and edit the sharing invitation.

3 Specify the permissions by selecting an appropriate access level from the Details list.

4 Click Send. Click Yes when prompted.

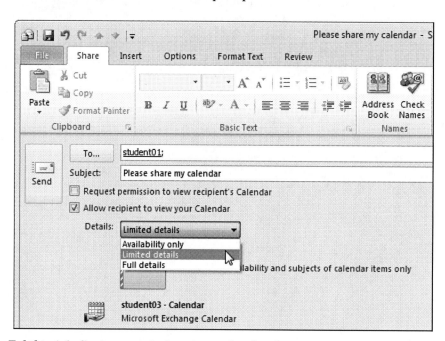

Exhibit 4-1: Setting permissions in a calendar sharing invitation

Calendar colors

Objective 5.3.2

If you frequently work with multiple calendars, you might find it helpful to change the color of the calendars. Doing so will make it easier for you to distinguish between them at a glance.

To change the color of an open calendar:

1 Right-click the calendar's tab.

2 Choose Color and then select a color from the gallery.

There is another method to change the color of your own calendar. You can also use this technique to set a color to be used for all calendars.

1 Open the Outlook Options dialog box.

2 In the left pane, click Calendar.

3 In the Display options section, click the color list button to display the colors gallery. Select the color you want to use.

4 Optional: Check "Use this color on all calendars." (Doing this will defeat the purpose of color-coding different calendars, however.)

5 Click OK.

Do it!

A-2: Sharing calendars

Here's how	Here's why
1 Right-click **Calendar**, as shown	▲ My Calendars ▦ Calendar
Choose **Share**, **Share Calendar**	To open a sharing invitation window.
2 Address the invitation to your partner	
3 From the Details list, choose **Limited details**	This grants your partner permission to see not only whether you're free or busy, but also the subjects of the items on your calendar.
4 Click **Send**	
Click **Yes**	
5 Activate Mail	
6 When your partner's message arrives, open it	
7 Click **Open this Calendar**	On the Ribbon. You are switched to Calendar view, and your partner's calendar is opened side by side with yours. Your partner's appointment is listed on his or her calendar.
8 In the Navigation pane, uncheck **Shared Calendars**	To hide your partner's calendar.
9 Show your partner's calendar	Check the box.
10 Right-click the tab of your partner's calendar	← Student02 ✕ Sun Mon
Point to **Color**	To display the colors gallery.
11 Click a color of your choice	▦ Automatic
	To change the calendar's color.

Objectives 5.3.3, 5.3.4

⚠ *If the partner's appointment isn't visible, delete the calendar group and have students repeat opening the calendar.*

Objective 5.3.2

Granting permissions

Explanation

You can manage another person's calendar or delegate management of yours by setting permissions on your calendar. This method of sharing does not grant permission to send e-mail (such as a meeting invite or response) on your behalf.

To grant someone permission to access your calendar:

1 Display your calendar. In the Navigation pane, under My Calendars, right-click Calendar and choose Properties to open the Calendar Properties dialog box.

2 Click the Permissions tab. Its options are shown in Exhibit 4-2.

3 In the Name list, select the name of the user to whom you're assigning permissions. If the name is not listed, click Add, select the name, click Add, and click OK.

4 From the Permission Level list, select the desired permission set. *Optional:* Directly assign more or fewer permissions by checking or clearing the boxes. In general, however, you should use the built-in permission levels instead.

5 Click OK to close the Calendar Properties dialog box.

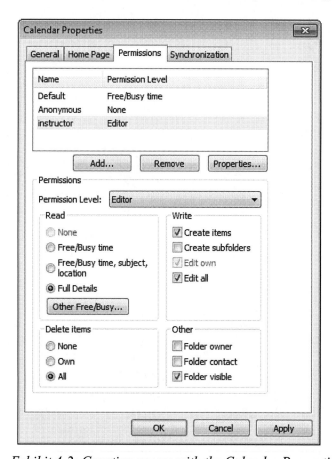

Exhibit 4-2: Granting access with the Calendar Properties dialog box

Groups and individuals

You can assign permissions to individuals or groups. Outlook recognizes the following types of individuals and groups:

- **Default** — The group that encompasses Outlook users not specifically granted other permissions.
- **Administrator** — The Outlook administrator. Although you can remove the Administrator from the permissions list, he or she can still access and manage the calendar from the Exchange Server.
- **Anonymous** — The group that encompasses non-Outlook users, those who are not logged in, or those outside your organization.
- *named_user* — A specific person. You can apply permissions to a specific user or users. Your user account is automatically granted the Owner permission level, even though it's not specifically listed.

Permission levels

The following table describes the permissions levels you can assign and the capabilities such levels permit. By default, folders inherit the permissions set on their parent folders.

Permission level	Grants permissions to...
Owner	Manage the calendar and its contents. The owner has full permissions, including the rights to set permissions for other users and manage the contact person for the calendar.
Publishing Editor	Create, read, edit, and delete items and subfolders. Cannot manage the permissions of other users. Can read all details about items on your calendar.
Editor	Create, read, edit, and delete items, but not subfolders. Can read all details about items on your calendar.
Publishing Author	Create, read, edit, and delete items and subfolders that he or she created. Cannot edit or delete items you created. Can read all details about items on your calendar.
Author	Same as Publishing Author, but cannot create subfolders.
Nonediting Author	Create items and read any item, but cannot edit any items.
Reviewer	Read all details about items on your calendar.
Contributor	Read your free/busy time, but no other details about your calendar items. Can create items on your calendar.
Free/Busy time, subject, location	Read your free/busy time, as well as the subject and location of items on your calendar. Cannot add to or edit your calendar.
Free/Busy time	Read your free/busy time. Cannot add to or edit your calendar.
None	Has no access to your calendar. You can set this permission level for the existing Default and Anonymous special groups, but not for any named users or real groups.

A-3: Permitting another user to manage your calendar

Here's how	Here's why
1 Right-click your calendar and choose **Properties…**	To open the Calendar Properties dialog box.
2 Click the **Permissions** tab	Because you shared your calendar with your partner in the previous activity, he or she is listed. Your partner has been granted a custom permission set.
Select your partner's name in the list	
3 From the Permission Level list, select **Editor**	
4 Click **OK**	To grant the permissions.
5 On the tab representing your partner's calendar, double-click his or her appointment	To open it. Because your partner granted you editing privileges, you can change this appointment.
6 Change the location to **987 Maple Ave**	
Click **Save & Close**	The changes might not be immediately reflected in Calendar view.
7 Clear the box for your partner's calendar	(In the Navigation pane.) To hide it.
Check your partner's calendar	To display it again. The updated location should now be visible.
8 Right-click **Shared Calendars** and choose **Delete Group**	
Click **Yes**	To delete the shared calendar from your Calendar folder.
9 Open the Properties dialog box for your calendar	
Click the **Permissions** tab	
10 Select your partner	
Click **Remove**	To revoke the permissions you had granted your partner.
Click **OK**	

Objective 5.3.3 (aligned with step 7)

Objective 5.3.4 (aligned with step 8)

Delegating access

Explanation

You can delegate access to your calendar and account to another user. In doing so, you grant that person permission to send messages on your behalf (as if he or she were you). You should check with your company management before delegating access.

To delegate access:

1   Click the File tab. Click Account Settings and choose Delegate Access.

2   Click Add. Select the user to whom you're delegating access, click Add, and click OK.

3   In the Delegate Permissions dialog box, shown in Exhibit 4-3, specify the permissions you're granting to this person. Optionally, check the boxes to send a summary message or to grant the person permission to see your private items.

4   Click OK twice.

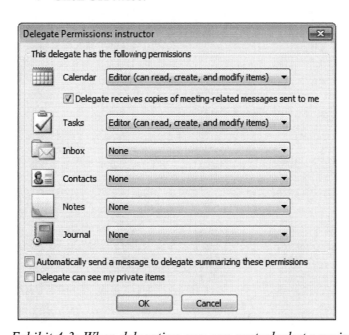

Exhibit 4-3: When delegating, you can control what permissions you're granting

Do it!

A-4:   Delegating access to your calendar

Here's how	Here's why
1 Click the **File** tab	
Click **Account Settings** and choose **Delegate Access**	To open the Delegates dialog box.
2 Click **Add**	To open the Add Users dialog box.
3 Select your partner	
Click **Add** and click **OK**	The Delegate Permissions dialog box opens.
4 Click **OK**	To accept the default permissions.
5 Click **OK**	To delegate access to your mailbox.
6 Open your calendar	If necessary.
7 Right-click **My Calendars**	
Choose **Add Calendar, From Address Book...**	
8 Select your partner	
Click **Calendar** and click **OK**	To add your partner's calendar to your Calendar view.
9 Right-click a free block on your partner's calendar	
Choose **New Meeting Request**	You'll book a meeting on your partner's calendar.
10 Address the request to yourself and the instructor	
In the Subject box, enter **Calendaring procedures**	
In the Location box, enter **Room A**	
Click **Send**	To send the invite.
11 Display your Inbox Observe the meeting invite	student01 1:49 PM Calendaring proceedures
	After a moment, the meeting invite is displayed. It is listed as coming from your partner even though you initiated the request.

Removing delegates

Explanation

To remove a delegate:

1 Click the File tab. Click Account Settings and choose Delegate Access.
2 Select the user from which you're removing access and click Remove.
3 Click OK.

Do it!

A-5:   Removing a delegate

Here's how	Here's why
1 Click the **File** tab	
Click **Account Settings** and choose **Delegate Access**	You will remove your partner as a delegate.
2 Select your partner	
3 Click **Remove**	You're not prompted for confirmation.
4 Click **OK**	To save your changes. Your partner is no longer a delegate for you and your account.

SharePoint calendars

Explanation

If your company uses SharePoint, you might have a calendar to maintain in that system in addition to your Outlook calendar. Fortunately, you can configure these two systems to work together so that you can view your two calendars side by side in Outlook. You can even drag appointments from one calendar to the other.

To enable SharePoint calendar viewing in Outlook:

1 Open Outlook.
2 In Internet Explorer, visit your SharePoint site.
3 Under Lists, click Calendar.
4 On the Ribbon, click the Calendar Tools | Calendar tab.
5 Click Connect to Outlook.
6 When prompted with the security alert, click Allow. Click Allow again.
7 In the Microsoft Outlook alert box, click Yes. The calendars are now displayed side by side in Outlook.

If you do not already have a SharePoint calendar, you can create one by following these steps.

1 From the Site Actions menu, choose More Options.
2 Click Calendar.
3 In the Name box, enter a name for your calendar.
4 Click Create.

Do it!

A-6: Accessing your SharePoint calendar in Outlook

Here's how	Here's why
1 Open Internet Explorer	Your SharePoint site should open (it was set as your home page during the setup for this course).
2 From the Site Actions menu, choose **More Options...**	If your Calendar list is already visible in the left pane, click it and skip to step 4 below.
Under Tracking, click **Calendar**	To access the Calendar creation page.
3 In the Name box, enter **SharePoint Calendar**	The Name box is in the right column.
Click **Create**	To create the Calendar list. It will now be available as a link on you're my Site page.
4 Click the **Calendar** tab, as shown	
5 Click **Connect to Outlook**	On the Calendar tab.
6 When prompted with the security alert, click **Allow**	
Click **Allow**	To acknowledge the second security alert.
7 Click **Yes**	To acknowledge the Outlook security alert box. Your calendar opens in Outlook. Your Outlook calendar is shown on the left; the SharePoint calendar is on the right.
8 Drag today's appointment from your Outlook calendar to your SharePoint calendar	
Click **Yes**	To acknowledge that incompatible content will not by copied.
9 Switch to Internet Explorer	
Press F5	To refresh the page. The appointment for today is now shown on your SharePoint calendar.
10 Close Internet Explorer	

On today's calendar, students should have an appointment that they created in an earlier activity.

Topic B: Managing contacts

Explanation

You can share contacts in much the same way you can share your calendar. You can use the Share Contacts button to share your contact list with another Outlook user. You can also grant access permissions to the user so that he or she can access your contacts directly.

To share your contacts:

1   Open your Contacts folder. In the Navigation pane, select the contact folder you want to share.

2   On the Home tab, in the Share group, click Share Contacts.

3   Address the sharing invitation, and optionally, change the subject to a message your recipient will find most meaningful. If you want to view the recipient's contacts, check the "Request permission" box.

4   Click Send and then Yes to deliver your invitation.

With this method, the recipient will be able to view your contacts, but not change them. He or she will be able to copy your contacts to his or her Contacts folder. You can enable more privileges by updating the sharing permissions in the contact folder's Properties dialog box.

Do it!

B-1:   Sharing contacts and Contacts folders

Here's how	Here's why
1 Activate Contacts	
2 In the Navigation pane, under My Contacts, select **Contacts**	You'll share your Contacts folder with your partner.

If necessary, have students input their area code when prompted.

Here's how	Here's why
3 Create a contact card, using fictitious information	

Doe, Jane

Jane Doe
Outlander Spices
Buyer

800-555-1212 Work
jane.doe@outlanderspices.com

1 Anystreet Rd.
Pleasantville, WA 98765

Here's how	Here's why
4 On the Home tab, in the Share group, click **Share Contacts**	
5 Enter your partner's address	
6 Click **Send**	To send the sharing invitation to your partner. He or she will send you one, so there's no need to check the Request permission box.
Click **Yes**	To confirm that you want to share your contacts with your partner in read-only mode.
7 Activate Mail	
8 When your partner's invitation arrives, open it	It might take a moment or two for the message to arrive.
9 Click **Open this Contacts folder**	On the Ribbon.
Close the invitation message window	

◢ My Contacts
    Suggested Contacts
    Contacts
    My Site
  Other Contacts
◢ Shared Contacts
    student02

Smith, Pat

Pat Smith
Outlander Spi
District Manag

pat.smith@ou

Your partner's contact list opens in your Contacts view.

If the contact is not visible, tell students to select a different contacts folder, and then their partner's shared contacts again.

Here's how	Here's why
10 Double-click the fictitious contact your partner created	To view the contact details. You have been granted full read-level access to the contact list.
Close the contact	

Exporting and importing contacts

Explanation

Another way to share contacts is to export your contact list. Your recipient can then import it into his or her mail program. You would use this method when sharing contacts with someone who doesn't use Outlook or with someone outside your organization. Of course, keep privacy and your company's policies in mind when sharing contact information.

Importing contacts was covered in the Outlook Intermediate course.

To export a list of contacts:

1 Click the File tab and then click Open.
2 Click Import.
3 Select "Export to a file" and click Next.
4 Select the type of file you want to export to and click Next.

   Comma Separated Values (DOS) is perhaps the most universal sharing format and is the best to choose when sharing with people who don't run Outlook, those who use a Web-based e-mail program, or those who don't run Windows.

5 Select the folder you want to export from (select Contacts to export your contact list). Click Next.
6 Click Browse. Enter a name for your exported file, and click OK.
7 Click Next and then click Finish.

Do it!

B-2: Exporting contacts

Here's how	Here's why
1 Click the **File** tab and click **Open**	
2 Click **Import**	
3 Select **Export to a file** and click **Next**	
4 Select **Comma Separated Values (DOS)** and click **Next**	To specify the file type.
5 Select **Contacts** and click **Next**	If necessary, to specify the folder to be exported.
6 Click **Browse**	
Enter **My contacts**	To specify a name for your file.
Click **OK**	
7 Click **Next**	
Click **Finish**	To export your contacts.
8 Click **Start** and choose **Documents**	To open your Documents folder. Your exported contacts file is in the folder. You could send it to a friend or co-worker as an attachment.
9 Close the Documents window	

SharePoint contacts

Explanation

You might have a list of contacts in SharePoint that you'd like to access from within Outlook. To do so, you must connect your SharePoint contact list to Outlook. The procedure for doing so is similar to viewing a SharePoint calendar within Outlook.

By default, a SharePoint 2010 My Sites page doesn't include a contact list. You can create one by following these steps:

1 From the Site Actions menu, choose More Options.
2 Click Contacts.
3 In the Name box, enter a name for your list.
4 Click Create.

Do it!

B-3: Creating a SharePoint contact list

Here's how	Here's why
1 Open Internet Explorer	Your SharePoint site should open (it was set as your home page during the setup for this course).
2 From the Site Actions menu, choose **More Options...**	
3 Click **Contacts**	
4 In the Name box in the right column, enter **SharePoint Contacts**	
5 Click **Create**	
6 Click **Add new item**	(In the body of the Web page.) You will create a fictitious contact so that you have something in this list to view in Outlook.
7 Enter these details as shown	

Last Name *	Pointe
First Name	Sherry
Full Name	Sherry Pointe
E-mail Address	sherry.pointe@outlanderspices.com

Click **Save**

Viewing SharePoint contact lists within Outlook

Explanation

To enable the ability to display your SharePoint contacts within Outlook:

1 Open Outlook.

2 In Internet Explorer, visit your SharePoint site.

3 In the top-right corner of the page, click your user name to display the menu, and choose My Site.

4 At the top of the page, click My Content.

5 On the left, under Lists, click your contact list's name.

6 On the Ribbon, click the List Tools | List tab.

7 Click Connect to Outlook.

8 When prompted with the security alert, click Allow. Click Allow again.

9 In the Microsoft Outlook alert dialog box, click Yes. Your SharePoint contact list is opened and displayed as a new contact folder within Outlook.

Do it!

B-4: Connecting your SharePoint contact list to Outlook

Here's how	Here's why

The contact list is already displayed because students just created it.

1 In Internet Explorer, click the **List** tab, as shown

If necessary.

2 Click **Connect to Outlook** — On the List Tools | List tab.

3 When prompted with the security alert, click **Allow**

Click **Allow** — To acknowledge the second security alert.

4 Click **Yes** — To acknowledge the Outlook security alert box. Your contact list is opened in Outlook. It is displayed as a contact folder.

5 Drag the **Sherry Pointe** contact to your Contacts folder — Click anywhere within the contact card and drag to the Contacts folder in the Navigation column.

6 Click **Contacts** — To display your Contacts folder. Sherry Pointe's card is listed in that folder.

7 Drag a contact from your Contacts folder to your SharePoint Contacts folder — To copy it to SharePoint.

Click **Yes** — To acknowledge that incompatible information won't be copied.

8 Switch to Internet Explorer

9 In the left column, click **SharePoint Contacts** — To refresh the list. Your Outlook contact is now included in this list

Unit summary: Calendars and contacts

Topic A   In this topic, you learned how to share your calendar with other people. You also set direct permissions to enable greater or lesser access to your calendar items. Then you learned how to delegate access to your calendar so that others can act on your behalf. Finally, you learned how to integrate your Outlook and SharePoint calendars.

Topic B   In this topic, you learned how to share your contacts. You exported lists of contacts as a means to share contacts with non-Outlook users. You then learned how to synchronize your contacts with SharePoint.

Independent practice activity

In this activity, you will practice working with both your SharePoint and Outlook calendars and contact lists.

1 Using Internet Explorer, create an appointment on your SharePoint calendar.

2 Copy that appointment from your SharePoint calendar to your Outlook calendar.

3 Using Internet Explorer, update the Sherry Pointe contact card in your SharePoint contact list (not the card you copied to Outlook). Change the address, title, or street address

4 From within Outlook, share your SharePoint contacts folder with your partner.

5 After your partner has shared it with you, open your partner's shared SharePoint contacts folder. Open your partner's Sherry Pointe contact card to view the changes he or she made.

6 Copy your partner's Sherry Pointe contact card to your Outlook Contacts group as a duplicate contact.

7 Close Internet Explorer.

Review questions

1 Outlook, in conjunction with Exchange Server, offers you three levels of shared calendar access. The levels are:

- *Sharing*

- *Setting calendar permissions*

- *Delegating access*

2 In addition to publishing your calendar to Office.com, Outlook enables you to publish your calendar to any _____-capable Web server.

   WebDAV

3 True or false? Within Outlook, calendar sharing is initiated by the person sharing his or her calendar, rather than by the person wanting access.

   True

4 Anyone granted Owner permissions has _____ access to his or her calendar or Contacts folder.

   full, or total

5 Describe a scenario in which you would delegate access to your calendar.

   To enable your administrative assistant to manage your calendar on your behalf, including sending and accepting meeting invitations.

6 You want to view your SharePoint calendar in Outlook. In which program do you initiate this sharing?

   SharePoint

7 True or false? You can share contact folders you create, but not your built-in Contacts folder.

   False. You can share your Contacts folder, too.

8 By default, when sharing contacts, recipients can _____ your contacts, but not _____ them.

   view, change

9 To export contacts, click the File tab and then click Open. Which button do you click next?

   A Export

   B Import

   C Save As

   D Account Settings

10 True or false? Once you've shared your SharePoint contacts with Outlook, the contact lists from both programs are displayed side by side or in overlay mode.

   False. Your SharePoint contacts appear as another contacts folder within Outlook.

Unit 5

Mail merges and templates

Unit time: 60 minutes

Complete this unit, and you'll know how to:

A Use the Mail Merge feature to send mass e-mail messages.

B Create templates that you can use to send similarly composed messages.

Topic A: Performing mail merges

Explanation

When you need to send an e-mail message to many recipients, you can save time by using Outlook's Mail Merge feature. Most of the text in the message will be identical for all recipients, but some specific elements—such as the recipient's name and address—will be different in each copy.

Unsolicited commercial e-mail

Better known as *spam* (that word is actually a trademark of the Hormel Foods Corp.), *unsolicited commercial e-mail (UCE)* is unwanted bulk e-mail traffic. It is illegal to send UCE in the United States and other countries. The CAN-SPAM Act of 2003 permits you to send UCE as long as the following conditions are met:

- You must provide a visible and operable means for recipients to opt out of future mailings, and you must process any opt-out requests within 10 days.

- The subject lines, the From names, and the content of your message must be accurate and relevant.

- You must include a legitimate physical address for your business.

- You cannot use "harvested" e-mail addresses (those you copy from Web sites or other directories), and you cannot falsify header information.

In general, e-mail messages that you send to existing customers are exempted from the CAN-SPAM act because they represent "normal" communications that are part of an existing "relationship." The law does not require you to get permission from existing customers. However, you should get permission from prospects and potential customers; you can do this through a sign-up form on your Web site, a checkbox on a physical mailing, and so forth.

Mail merge limitations

Outlook does not handle all phases of the mail merge on its own. You must use it in conjunction with Word. You select the contacts to e-mail in Outlook, and compose your form letter in Word. Outlook then sends the messages. This means that you can't use Outlook's mail merge functions if you don't have Word installed or if its mail merge features are disabled.

Outlook's mail merging function is suitable for small, occasional mailings. It is not meant for regular mass communication campaigns, such as newsletters, sale announcements, and so forth. For those types of mailings, you should use a dedicated mass mailing application or service, such as Constant Contact.

Do it!   **A-1:   Importing contacts to use in a mail merge**

The files for this activity are in Student Data folder **Unit 5\Topic A**.

Here's how	Here's why
1 Activate Contacts	
2 Under My Contacts, right-click **Contacts** and choose **New Folder...**	
3 In the Name box, type **Customers**	To name the folder.
Click **OK**	To create a folder for storing your mail merge contacts.
4 Click the **File** tab and click **Open**	
5 Click **Import**	
6 With **Import from another program or file** selected, click **Next**	
7 Select **Comma Separated Values (Windows)** and click **Next**	To specify the type of file to be imported.
8 Click **Browse**	
Navigate to the current topic's folder	Student Data folder Unit 5\Topic A.
Select **Key customers** and click **OK**	To specify the file to be imported.
Click **Next**	
9 Scroll up and select **Customers**	To specify the folder into which you'll import the contacts.
Click **Next**	
10 Click **Finish**	To import the contacts.
11 In the Navigation pane, select **Customers**	(If necessary.) To view the contacts you have imported. Fictitious names, titles, companies, and other details have been paired with the student e-mail addresses that you and your classmates have been using.

Explain that students will send a mail merge to their classmates and see how they can include personalized details in their messages.

Steps in a mail merge

Explanation

To access the Mail Merge command in Outlook, activate the Contacts folder. From there, follow these basic steps to perform a mail merge in Outlook:

1   Select the contacts you want to e-mail (Shift+click or Ctrl+click to select multiple contacts).

2   In the Actions group on the Home tab, click Mail Merge.

3   Specify mail merge options in the Mail Merge Contacts dialog box, shown in Exhibit 5-1. You can use this dialog box to specify whether to create a document or open an existing Word document. In the Merge options section, you can specify whether to create a form letter, mailing labels, envelopes, and so forth.

   To create an e-mail message, specify these settings:

   • Document type: Form Letters

   • Merge to: E-mail

   • Subject: Enter the subject for your e-mail message

4   Click OK in the Mail Merge Contacts dialog box to open Microsoft Word. When composing your message, you can insert a *merge field*, which will be replaced by data from your Contacts list when your message is sent. Exhibit 5-2 illustrates merge fields in a document, while Exhibit 5-3 shows a preview of a message with actual data shown in place of the fields.

5   In the Finish group on the Mailings tab (in Word), click Finish & Merge.

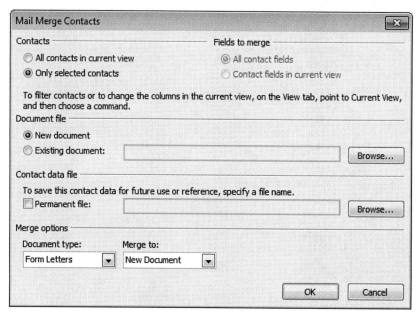

Exhibit 5-1: Setting options in the Mail Merge Contacts dialog box

> Dear «First Name»:
>
> As «Job Title» at «Company», you know that great spices are critical to great food. But how do you know which spices to use to best enhance the flavors of your recipes? How much spice is enough and how much is too much? Which foods and drinks will best fit with your spiced dish? Outlander Spices is proud to announce our new monthly *Spice Sampler Club*. Club members receive these great benefits:
>
> - Free packets of sample spices every month
> - Recipe ideas and tips

Exhibit 5-2: A document containing merge fields

> Dear Danny:
>
> As Executive Chef at The Wellesley, you know that great spices are critical to great food. But how do you know which spices to use to best enhance the flavors of your recipes? How much spice is enough and how much is too much? Which foods and drinks will best fit with your spiced dish? Outlander Spices is proud to announce our new monthly *Spice Sampler Club*. Club members receive these great benefits:
>
> - Free packets of sample spices every month
> - Recipe ideas and tips

Exhibit 5-3: A document after merging with a recipient list

Do it!

A-2:   Creating a mail merge

The files for this activity are in Student Data folder **Unit 5\Topic A**.

Here's how	Here's why
1 Press ⟨CTRL⟩ + ⟨A⟩	To select all contacts in the Customers folder.
2 On the Home tab, in the Actions group, click **Mail Merge**	To open the Mail Merge Contacts dialog box.
3 Under Contacts, verify that **Only selected contacts** is selected	To send your message to the contacts you selected.
4 Select **Existing document**	
Click **Browse** and navigate to the current topic folder	The topic folder should be displayed by default.
Select **Spice sampler club** and click **OK**	
5 Under Merge options, verify that Document type is set to **Form Letters**	
From the Merge to list, select **E-mail**	You will merge to an e-mail message rather than to a printed document or other target.
In the Message subject line box, type **Announcing the Spice Sampler Club**	
6 Click **OK**	Microsoft Word opens and the document is loaded.

Inserting merge fields

Explanation

A *merge field* is a placeholder for data that can change. For example, you can use a field to insert a date that is automatically updated, so the current date is always shown. Contact details from your address book are also available as merge fields.

To insert a field:

1 In Word, click the Mailings tab.
2 In the Write & Insert Fields group, click Insert Merge Field. To insert contact details, select Address Fields. The resulting dialog box is shown in Exhibit 5-4.
3 Select the field you want to insert.
4 Click Insert.

In the document, fields are shaded gray when they're selected. Each field has a *field code*, which is the underlying instruction that provides the necessary result. Such field codes are normally hidden, though you can display them by modifying Word's options.

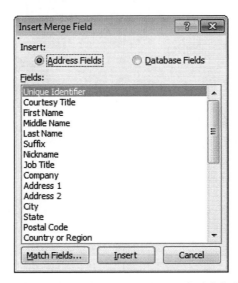

Exhibit 5-4: The Insert Merge Field dialog box, showing address fields

Do it!

A-3:   Inserting a merge field

The files for this activity are in Student Data folder **Unit 5\Topic A**.

Here's how	Here's why
1 In Word, observe the document	It contains a mix of text and merge codes, which are surrounded by the guillemets (double angle brackets, « »).
2 On the Mailings tab, click **Preview Results**	(In the Preview Results group.) Field codes are replaced by the data from your first contact.
Click **Preview Results**	To display the field codes again.
3 Place the insertion point between «Job Title» and the comma that follows	As «Job Title⌶ you to use to best enha You'll add new text and a field code here.
4 Press (SPACEBAR), type **at**, and press (SPACEBAR)	As «Job Title» at , you spices to use to best e
5 In the Write & Insert Fields group, click where indicated	Insert Merge Field ▾ (Click the top part of the button.) To open the Insert Merge Field dialog box.
Select **Address Fields**	To narrow the list of fields to those available from Outlook, as shown in Exhibit 5-4.
Select **Company**	
Click **Insert** and then click **Close**	
6 Click **Insert Merge Field**, as shown	Insert Merge Field ▾ (Click the bottom part of the button.) To display a drop-down list of fields. This list matches the larger "Database Fields" list that you saw in the Insert Merge Field dialog box.
Press (ESC)	To close the list.

7 Click **Preview Results**

> Dear Danny:
>
> As Executive Chef at The Wellesley, y
> know which spices to use to best enh

You've added the field code for the company name, which is replaced by the contact's specific information.

Click **Preview Results**

To show the merge codes again.

Finishing and merging

Explanation

After you have composed your message and entered your merge fields, you're ready to process the mailing. In Word, click the Finish & Merge button on the Mailings tab and choose Send E-mail Messages to open the Merge to E-mail dialog box, shown in Exhibit 5-5.

Exhibit 5-5: Setting final mailing options before sending your merged document

The following table describes the options you can set in the Merge to E-mail dialog box.

Option	Used to...
To list	Specify which field contains the recipient's e-mail address. You might use its options to send to your recipients' second or other alternate addresses.
Subject	Set or alter the subject line here.
Mail format	Specify whether to send an HTML (formatted) message, plain text, or send your document as an attachment to a plain text message.
Send records	Specify which recipients to send to (all, current recipient, or a numbered range).

Do it!

A-4: Sending the merged message

Here's how	Here's why
1 On the Mailings tab, in the Finish group, click **Finish & Merge**	In Word.
Choose **Send E-mail Messages...**	
2 Observe the options in the Merge to E-mail dialog box	You can select which field contains the recipient's e-mail address, the subject line, and so forth.
3 Click **OK**	The Word document remains open. Your cursor will change to the busy indicator (spinning circle) as each message is sent. You might receive one or more pop-up status messages in the lower-right corner of your screen as messages are delivered.
4 Close Word	
Click **Don't Save**	To abandon changes you made in the Word document.
5 Activate Mail	
6 Open a copy of the message you received	Your student address was included in the imported list, so you should receive copies from each of the other students in class plus from your own mailing.
Observe the message	The fictitious name and data assigned to your contact have been merged into the form letter.
Close the message	

Only the first six students in your class will receive the message.

Topic B: Working with templates

Explanation

Do you have to submit a weekly timesheet, or submit expense reports to request reimbursement? You could simply type the entire message each time. More likely, you turn to other programs such as Excel spreadsheets or Word documents to create report templates. Outlook provides a means for you to create templates that can form the basis for your regular mailings.

To create an e-mail template, follow these steps:

1   Compose a new message, entering any information that will be common to all future instances of messages based on your template.

2   Optional: Insert fields, such as dates, that can be updated automatically by Outlook.

3   Save the file as a template.

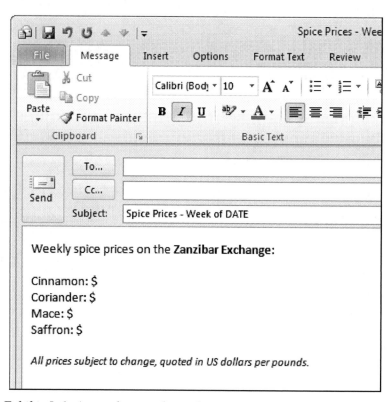

Exhibit 5-6: A sample e-mail template

Do it!

B-1: Creating an e-mail template

Here's how	Here's why
1 Activate Mail	If necessary.
2 Compose a new message, as shown in Exhibit 5-6	Make sure to add the bold, italics, and smaller font size to match the exhibit.
3 Click the **File** tab and then click **Save As**	
4 From the Save as type list, select **Outlook Template**	To specify that you want to save the message as a template.
5 Click **Save**	To save your template.
6 Close the message without saving	

Showing the Developer tab

Explanation

One way to use a template you have created involves using buttons on the Developer tab. That tab is not visible by default. To display it, you need to open the Outlook Options dialog box, show the Customize Ribbon options, and check the Developer box.

Do it!

B-2: Showing the Developer tab

Here's how	Here's why
1 Right-click the **Home** tab and choose **Customize the Ribbon...**	To open the Outlook Options dialog box directly to the Ribbon options.
2 In the Main Tabs list, check **Developer**	☑ View / ☑ Developer / ☑ Add-Ins To show the Developer tab.
3 Click **OK**	To close the Outlook Options dialog box.
4 Click the **Developer** tab	This tab provides buttons that enable you to design your own forms or modify existing forms.

Applying an e-mail template

Explanation

To use a template, you must apply it to your message. However, you don't do this as you might with Microsoft Word or another program. Outlook provides two means to apply a template to a message:

- In Windows Explorer, double-click the template (*.oft) file. Outlook will open (if it's not already open), and a new message window based on your template will also open.

- In Outlook, on the Developer tab, click Choose Form to open the Choose Form dialog box, shown in Exhibit 5-7. By specifying the source of the form as your templates, you can open your template and create an e-mail message based on it.

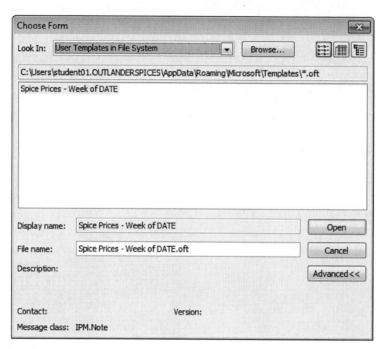

Exhibit 5-7: Using the Choose Form dialog box to create an e-mail message based on a template

Do it!

B-3: Sending a message based on a template

Here's how	Here's why
1 On the Developer tab, click **Choose Form**	To open the Choose Form dialog box, shown in Exhibit 5-7.
2 From the Look In list, select **User Templates in File System**	By default, Outlook scans the standard Templates directory, where you saved your template file. It should be listed in the box.
3 Select **Spice Prices – Week of DATE**	
4 Click **Open**	A message window opens, with the text you entered into your template already filled in.
5 Address the message to your partner	
Replace DATE with today's date	
Update the prices as shown	Cinnamon: $2.95 Coriander: $4.70 Mace: $2.45 Saffron: $284.00
6 Send the message	

Fields and objects

You can add fields, pictures, and objects to your template. For example, you can add a field code that will be replaced with the current date and time each time you create a message based on your template. You can add a picture that is included with every message based on the template.

Use the commands on the Insert tab to add fields, pictures, and other items to your template. Such field codes must be in the message body (not in the Subject or To boxes, for example).

Do it!

B-4: Adding a field code to your template

Here's how	Here's why
1 Using the Choose Form button, open your template	Click Choose Form, look in User Templates, select your template, and click Open.
2 Place the insertion point before the period in the last line of the message	After the words "per pounds."
3 Type **as of**	
4 Click the **Insert** tab	
5 In the Text group, click **Date & Time**	
6 Select the second date format, as shown	Available formats: 6/30/2010 Wednesday, June 30, 2010 June 30, 2010 The date shown on your screen will differ from what's shown here.
7 Check **Update automatically**	
8 Click **OK**	
9 Save the message as an Outlook Template, overwriting the earlier version you created	Click the File tab and click Save As, specify the file type as Outlook Template, click Save, and click Yes.
10 Close the message without saving	
11 Compose a new message based on your template	(Click Choose Form, look in User Templates, select your template, and click Open.) A new message window opens, this time containing the date.
12 Point to the date in the message	ds as of Wednesday June 30, 2010. It is shaded gray as you point to it, indicating that it is a field code.
13 Close the message	Without sending.

Unit summary: Mail merges and templates

Topic A   In this topic, you learned how to send mass e-mail messages by using the **Mail Merge** feature. You added **merge fields** to a form letter in Word, merged it with a recipient list, and sent the resulting e-mail messages.

Topic B   In this topic, you learned how to create **message templates** that you can use to send repetitive messages. You saved a message as a template file and then used the template to compose a message. Then, you added a **field code** to your template, which was updated when you created a message based on that template.

Independent practice activity

In this activity, you will open and modify a template file. Then you'll use it to send a message to your partner.

The files for this activity are in Student Data folder **Unit 5\Unit summary**.

1 Open Windows Explorer.

2 Navigate to the current unit's folder, and open the Unit Summary folder. Double-click the **Timesheet** file.

3 Address the resulting Outlook message to your partner.

4 Complete the timesheet, using fictitious data. An example of a completed message is shown in Exhibit 5-8.

5 Send a message to your partner. When it arrives, open the message sent to you by your partner.

6 Close all open windows and Outlook.

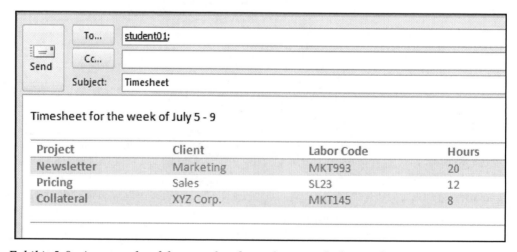

Timesheet for the week of July 5 - 9

Project	Client	Labor Code	Hours
Newsletter	Marketing	MKT993	20
Pricing	Sales	SL23	12
Collateral	XYZ Corp.	MKT145	8

Exhibit 5-8: An example of the completed template, ready for sending

Review questions

1 True or false? Outlook manages all stages of a mail merge operation.

False. You compose the message in Microsoft Word.

2 What's the first step to perform a mail merge in Outlook?

Select the contacts to whom you want to send the e-mail message.

3 What is a merge field?

It is a placeholder for live data that will be inserted when your mail merge is processed.

4 When you're composing your mail merge document, which button do you click to temporarily view live data in place of the merge fields?

A Preview Results

B Preflight

C View Live Data

D View Sample

5 True or false? You can use Outlook (and Word) to create a mail merge that you print rather than send by e-mail.

True.

6 What is the purpose of a template?

Templates provide consistent text and formatting that can be used to create an Outlook item, such as a message that you send often.

7 What is the procedure to save a message as a template?

a *Open the message that you want to save as a template.*

b *Click the File tab and click Save As.*

c *From the Save as type list, select Outlook Template.*

d *In the File name box, enter a name.*

e *Click Save.*

8 True or false? Templates can contain formatting, such as bold text, pictures, tables, and so forth.

True

9 Describe the two means of composing a message based on a template.

• *In Windows Explorer, double-click the template (*.oft) file.*

• *On the Developer tab, click Choose Form. From the Look In list, select User Templates in File System. Select your template and click Open.*

10 How do you display the Developer tab?

Use the Customize Ribbon settings in the Outlook Options dialog box.

Course summary

This summary contains information to help you bring the course to a successful conclusion. Using this information, you will be able to:

A Use the summary text to reinforce what students have learned in class.

B Direct students to the next courses in this series (if any), and to any other resources that might help students continue to learn about Microsoft Outlook.

Topic A: Course summary

At the end of the class, use the following summary text to reinforce what students have learned. It is intended not as a script, but rather as a starting point.

Unit summaries

Unit 1

Students learned how to stay current with the activities of colleagues on **social networks,** such as SharePoint. They subscribed to **RSS** news feeds and read articles within a feed.

Unit 2

Students learned how to **manage their mailboxes** by deleting old and unneeded messages, deleting the contents of automatic folders, and compacting their mailboxes. Students also **archived** messages to local files and the archive mailbox.

Unit 3

Students created, forwarded, and customized **notes**; created automatic and manual **Journal** entries; and opened and modified Journal entries.

Unit 4

Students shared access to their **calendar** with others by granting varying levels of permissions. Students accessed their **SharePoint calendar** in Outlook. Then they **shared contacts** with others, exported contacts, and accessed SharePoint contacts in Outlook.

Unit 5

Students sent personalized e-mail messages by using the **Mail Merge** feature. Then they created **templates** and sent messages based on those templates.

Topic B: Continued learning after class

Point out to your students that it is impossible to learn how to use any software effectively in a single day. To get the most out of this class, students should begin working with the advanced Outlook techniques they learned to perform real tasks as soon as possible. We also offer resources for continued learning.

Next courses in this series

This is the last course in this series.

Other resources

For more information, visit www.axzopress.com.

Glossary

Archive mailbox

A special mailbox, associated with your account, in which you can store archived messages and items. Items in this mailbox don't count toward your primary mailbox's quota.

Archiving

The process of storing old messages in a separate file on your computer or in a special archive mailbox on the Exchange server.

Delegate

The person granted permissions to perform tasks on behalf of another user.

Journal

An Outlook feature that enables you to track the work you perform in relation to contacts, messages, and documents.

Mail merge

A feature used to send many personalized messages, based on a single starting document, to many contacts.

Merge field

A placeholder for actual data that will be inserted when a mail-merge message is sent.

Notes

An Outlook feature you can use to jot down reminders, useful ideas, and other information that you can refer to later.

Outlook Social Connector (OSC)

An Outlook feature that displays, in the People Pane, updates and information from colleagues on a social network.

Quota

A storage limit placed on your mailbox.

RSS (Really Simple Syndication)

A standard means for content producers to publish news and information on the Web. RSS uses XML files in a standardized format to disseminate this information.

RSS aggregator

A client software program used to read RSS feeds. More commonly called a "reader."

RSS feed

A delivery mechanism for Web content distributed in XML format, allowing users to monitor multiple sources of news, Web logs (blogs), and other content that is updated frequently.

SharePoint

A collaboration and communication software tool published by Microsoft.

Templates

Sample documents that provide consistent text and formatting that you can use to create Outlook items, such as a message that you send often.

Index